Visible

A play by Sarah Woods

A co-commission by the Royal Shakespeare Company and Cardboard Citizens
First performed on 16 March 2006 at Contact Theatre, Manchester

Cast

(in order of appearance)

Rob / Neil Rory MacGregor
Hattie Karen Paullada
Alex Patrick Onione
Stuart White Gus Brown
Catherine Antonia Coker
Peter Tilson Jake Goode
Sugar, Honey, Treacle The Company
Lillian Sylvia Larry
Bashkim Agron Biba

Creative Team

Director Adrian Jackson
Designer Rajha Shakiry
Lighting Designer Emma Chapman
Composer Anders Södergren

Assistant Director Sarah Levinsky
Fight Director Kevin Rowntree
Video Gavin Bush

Production

Producer Kate Sarley
Production Manager Simon Curtis
Tour Consultant Vanessa Stone
Company Stage Manager Louise Tischler
Technical Stage Manager Dominic Bell
Casting Agent Hannah Miller, with Janine Snape
Costume Supervisor Jools Osbourne
Tour Marketing & Press Helen Snell Ltd (020 7287 6889)

Production Credits

English Touring Theatre Rehearsal Space
Additional Production Management by Jonathan Yeoman
Costume Makers Ida Ravn and Amanda Price
Set Builder Andy Stubbs
Scene Painter Sarah Crane
Mark Wilshire at Set-Up
Le Creuset
www.bigfoto.com
www.gallery.hd.org

For Cardboard Citizens

Tim Arthur *Associate Director*
Mal Bassi *Circus Workshop Leader*
Simon Black *Fundraising Coordinator*
Penny Cliff *Writing for Performance Workshop Leader*
Clara Clint *Project Manager: This Way Up*
Jo De Waal *Singing Workshop Leader*
Jo Gallagher *Learning & Employment Officer*
Ben Henshall *Samba Workshop Leader*
Adrian Jackson *Artistic Director*
Ewelina Kolaczek *Admin Assistant / Training Coordinator*
Shelley McLennan *Project Assistant: This Way Up*
Terry O'Leary *Associate Artist*
Richard Oyarzabal *Executive Director*
Natalie Poulton *Fundraising and Marketing Assistant*
Naomi Selwyn *Project Manager: Engagement Programme*
Jo Taylor *Office Manager & Production Co-ordinator for VISIBLE*
Louise Wallington *Progression and Support Manager*
Charlotte Woodward *Project Assistant*
Hannah Wysome *Regional Development, Coordinator, NW*
Reynaldo Young *New Music Ensemble Workshop Leader*
Board Members Neil Churchill, Mary Ann Hushlak, Mary Blackwell, Dan Mace,
Gaynor Quilter, Sian Edwardes-Evans, Mark Thompson
www.cardboardcitizens.org.uk

Special Thanks to

Micheline Steinberg, Hannah Miller, Fred Meller, John Ramm, Simon Trinder,
Sian Brooke, Mojisola Adebayo, Katherine Kelly, Jon Revell, Martin Wady,
Andrew M Bailey, Matt Osborne, Anna Bliss Scully, Barry Saltman,
Ginny Osborne

Company Biographies

Rory MacGregor *Rob / Neil*

Rory has just finished filming his fourth series on *Spooks* where he played computer genius, Colin Wells. Rory's film credits include: Dubonet Warrior in *Gladiatress*; Sound Engineer in *Love Actually* and NASA Scientist in *Thunderpants*. His television credits include: Doctor in *Casanova* (BBC), Colin Wells in *Spooks* (Series I-IV); *My Family* (BBC); Ted in *Black Books* (Channel 4); Mort the Mortician in *Lexx* (Channel 5/Silver Light); PC Waterhouse in *Bad Girls* (ITV) and Andrew Stokes in *Hollyoaks* (Channel 4). His theatre credits include: Cassius in *Julius Caesar* (Hull Truck Theatre); *Early Morning* (National Theatre Studio); Sir Benjamin Backbite in *School for Scandal* (Demirep Independent); and most recently Mr Charrington/Smye in *1984* (Hull Truck Theatre).

Karen Paullada *Hattie*

Karen trained at LAMDA. Her theatre credits include: *Pendragon* (National Youth Music Theatre); *Ubu Roi* and *Animal Farm* (National Youth Theatre of Wales); Married Woman and Actress in *The Blue Room* (Diorama Arts Centre/Tour); Liz in *Blond Bombshells of 1943* (The West Yorkshire Playhouse); Beauty in *Beauty and the Beast* (RSC); Mared in *Cancer Time* (Latchmere Theatre/503); Cinderella in *Cinderella* (Oxford Playhouse). Television credits include: *Hearts of Gold* (BBC); *The Second Quest* (YTV); *The Green Green Grass* (BBC).

Patrick Onione *Alex*

Patrick was born and brought up in London. He has worked with Cardboard Citizens for three years.

Productions include: *Reaching Crisis Points* (Labour Party Conference), *Flying into Sunset* by Noel Greig (London and national schools tour), *The Man with Size 12 Feet* by Adrian Jackson (hostels and theatres tour), and *Woyzeck* by Georg Büchner (Riverside Studios and touring).

Gus Brown *Stuart*

Theatre credits include: *Laurence & Gus: Men In Love* (Birmingham Rep); *A History Of The World In Five & A Half Sketches* (Edinburgh); *The Blue Diamond of Askabar* (Changeling Theatre); *The Waves* (Passepartout/BAC); *All Will Become Clear* (Soho Theatre); *Eurydice* (Whitehall Theatre); *Design For Living* (ETT/UK Tour); *The Winter's Tale* (Russia Tour 96/Cambridge). Television credits include: *Green Wing*; *Broken News*; *Tynan – In Praise of Hardcore*; *The Robinsons*; *The All New Harry Hill Show*; *Dave Gorman's Important Astrology Experiment*; *My Hero*; *Fun At The Funeral Parlour*; *Daydream Believers*; *Chambers*; *The Mitchell & Webb Situation*; *Happiness*. Film credits include: *That Girl From Rio*. Radio credits include: *Laurence & Gus: Untold Stories, What A Carve Up!, Rigor Mortis* (BBC Radio Four).

Antonia Coker *Catherine*

Antonia Coker has worked in theatre nationally and internationally for the past 22 years. Most recent theatre includes: *It's Just A Name* by Don Kinch (Birmingham Rep.), *In the Parlour with the Ladies* by Nona Shepherd (Drill hall), *Lear's Daughters* by Women's Theatre Group, Yellow Earth (national tour and Soho Theatre), *Ragamuffin* by Armani Naphtali (Theatre Royal Brighton and Birmingham Rep.), and *The Big Life* by Paul Sirett, Theatre Royal Stratford East, which transferred to the West End Apollo Theatre, Shaftsbury Avenue. Having worked with many theatre in education companies, she continues to work with various youth theatres. She has also had the pleasure of working on, *Things Fall Apart* by Chinua Achebe adapted by Biyi Bandele with collective artists directed by Chuck Mike.

Jake Goode *Peter Tilson*

Jake Goode has been a street performer for 12 years. In 1999 he founded Other Half Productions with his partner Jo Galbraith. They have developed several diverse acts for all types of events, audiences and media and have completed commissions for the National Street Arts Festival and the Millennium Dome amongst others. Their acts have been booked on five continents and they have toured for the British Council. Jake has been working with Cardboard Citizens almost since it was founded, appearing in *A Woman of No Importance*, *Flat 4D*, *Short Circuit*, *The Beggars Opera*, *Mincemeat* and *Pericles*. Jake is a visiting lecturer at the Circus Space, and teaches circus workshops for Cirque du Monde, the charitable wing of Cirque du Soleil. He lives in Hackney with his partner and five year old son.

Adrian Jackson *Director*

Adrian Jackson is Artistic Director of Cardboard Citizens. Past productions for the company include *King* by Penny Cliff after John Berger, *Pericles* by William Shakespeare (with RSC), *Woyzeck* by Georg Büchner, *Mincemeat* by Adrian Jackson, and *Farhana Sheikh*, *Going Going Gone*, *Home and Away* and *Dick and his Dog* by Adrian Jackson, *The Beggar's Opera* adapted from John Gay (with ENO Bayliss Programme),

The Lower Depths by Maxim Gorky (with London Bubble); as writer, *The Man with Size 12 Feet*. For London Bubble, *Too Much Too Young* by Catherine Johnson, *Once Upon a Time Far Far Away* by Farhana Sheikh and *Dealing with Feelings* by Jonathan Petherbridge. For Crisis, *Under the Heavens* (Shakespeare's Globe). He is the translator of five books by Augusto Boal and an expert on Forum Theatre. He has taught The Theatre of the Oppressed in development and educational contexts around the world, including South Africa, Namibia, Mauritius, Ireland, Finland, Hong Kong, Colombia and Eastern Europe.

Rajha Shakiry *Designer*

Studied at Wimbledon School of Art. Stage and Costume designs include: *Everything is Illuminated* (Etcetera). *Goblin Market* (Southwark Playhouse), *King, The Wall, Changes* and *Love Wars* for Cardboard Citizens, *Tales From the Emerald City* for ShowHow, *Nymphs and Shepherds* (Etcetera Theatre), *Don Giovanni* and *Le Nozze di Figaro* (Beauforthuis, Holland), *Brokenville* (Oval House Theatre), *Tomorrow Never Knows* and *Chasing* (Hen & Chickens). Co-design *The Ghost Downstairs* (New Perspectives Theatre, Mansfield). As Assistant Designer with Fred Meller *The Fever* (Theatre 503), *Woyzeck* (Riverside Studios), with Francis O'Connor *Peter Pan* (Savoy Theatre), with Michael Pavelka *Rose Rage* (Theatre Royal Haymarket), with Anthony Lamble *Don Juan* (Gatehouse Theatre), *Dancing at Lughnasa* (NYT). Rajha also freelances in the puppets department at *The Lion King* and has assisted in producing large-scale costumes for the Notting Hill Carnival for over five years.

Emma Chapman
Lighting Designer

Emma has been working as a freelance Lighting Designer since completing her technical training at Bristol Old Vic Theatre School. Her theatre credits include: *Beautiful Thing* (Sound Theatre), *Jack and the Beanstalk* (Sheffield Lyceum), *The Railway Children* and *Wind in the Willows* (Sevenoaks Playhouse), *Phaedra's Love* (Bristol Old Vic and The Barbican), *The Pied Piper* (Opera North Education), *Impermanence* (Purcell Room and Touring), *London Talent 2005* (Shaw Theatre, London), *Manchester Arts Education Initiative* (Contact Theatre, Manchester), *Riders to the Sea* (Southwark Playhouse), *Smilin' Through* (Birmingham Rep/Contact Theatre), *Collision* (Birmingham Stage Company), *Cinderella* (PWC, Peacock Theatre/Wakefield Theatre Royal), *Wind in the Willows* (Bloomsbury Theatre/Clear Channel Tour), *Io Passions* (Relight, Almeida Opera), *Twelfth Night* (Associate Lighting Designer/Relighter, ETT), *Attempts on her Life* (BAC), *Markings* (Attic Theatre Company), *Buzz* (Sgript Cymru), *Young Emma* and *Something Cloudy, Something Clear* (Finborough Theatre), *The Nest* (UK Tour), *Descent* (The Door, Birmingham Rep), *Four Toys in a Tent* (New Vic Studio, Bristol Old Vic), *High Society* (Aberystwyth Arts Centre/Swansea Grand), *It Takes Ages to Be This Good, The Birds, Airwaves, Wasps, The Love of a Nightingale* and *Dr. Prospero* (Salberg Studio, Salisbury Playhouse), *A Tale of Two Cities* (Main House, Salisbury Playhouse).

Anders Södergren
Composer

Anders has composed widely in theatre, film, television and radio. He began as a composer and musical director in theatre in Sweden and has since worked for many companies including the Royal Shakespeare Company, BBC, Channel 4, ITV, and Canal+. His recent work includes *Soap* (The Stephen Joseph Theatre), *Daughter of the Air* (RSC &BBC R3) *Back to Methuselah* (RSC Stratford and Barbican), *Antigone* (Citizens Theatre Glasgow), *Katherine Howard* (Chichester Festival Theatre), *Disposing of the Body* (Hampstead Theatre), *The Tailor of Gloucester* (BBC R3), *This Old House* (BBC 2 Drama). His work as assistant composer/arranger with Oscar-winner Stephen Warbeck includes the films: *Billy Elliot, Mrs Brown, The Mystery Men, Charlotte Gray* and *The Hours*.

Sarah Levinsky
Assistant Director

Sarah is Co-Director and founding member of Mapping4D theatre company. With Mapping4D she has directed *Slender* (BAC), *The Pink Bits* (Riverside Studios, winner 2004 Oxford Samuel Beckett Theatre Trust Award), *Vertigo* and *Little English* (both Camden People's Theatre). Other directing: *Lost in Peru* by Ben Yeoh (Camden People's Theatre). As performer/deviser: *100 Years in Boxes: As Worlds Fall Apart* (dir. Richard Gough, Centre for Performance Research); research and development work with El Baldio Teatro, Argentina. Workshop leader for Cardboard Citizens, Attic Theatre Company, and Company of Angels.

Sarah Woods
Writer

Sarah's translation of *Hilda* by Marie NDiaye opens at the Hampstead Theatre this April, while her adaptation of Roald Dahl's *Fantastic Mr Fox* plays at Polka Childrens' Theatre, after five star reviews at The Little Angel.

Sarah is currently writing *One Day in the Future*, a 'monsterist' play for Playbox and a new version of *Timon of Athens* (Cardboard Citizens/RSC Complete Works Festival).

Other plays include *Only Fools* (Contemporary Clowning Projects, with Angela de Castro), *Walking On Water* (Theatre Centre); *Cake* (Jade Theatre Company); *Soap* (Stephen Joseph Theatre); *Antigone* (Tag Theatre Co. Glasgow) selected as a finalist of the Susan Smith Blackburn Prize 2001; *Trips* (Birmingham Rep); and *Grace* (Jade Theatre Company) nominated for the LWT Comedy Writing Award at the 1997 Edinburgh Festival.

For TV, *The World of the Impressionists* (BBC1) is scheduled for Spring 2006, as is *If…the Oil Runs Out* (BBC 2/Discovery). For Radio, Sarah has written over thirty original plays, adaptations and series. For Opera, a new version of *Fidelio* for Graham Vick's Birmingham Opera production.

Sarah is a member of the Monsterists, and also runs Birmingham University's Mphil(B) in Playwriting.

Visible
Director's Note

Cardboard Citizens is renowned for its Forum Theatre work with homeless people as performers and audiences, on and off stage, in hostels and day centres around the country; VISIBLE will be the company's first full-scale venture into the regular theatre touring circuit. To move from the one environment to the other without compromising the company's preference for making challenging work that engages with its audiences, was always going to be a tall order. After discussions with the RSC on how to continue our fruitful collaboration, following on from the success of the site-specific co-production of PERICLES, I was introduced to the work of various contemporary writers, and Sarah Woods stood out amongst them as a playwright not afraid to take risks and break rules – so we commissioned her for this tour.

The first outing for VISIBLE (co-commisioned with the RSC) was to be its performance as a reading at the New Work festival in Stratford and Soho. In these circumstances, working with a company drawn equally from the ranks of Cardboard Citizens and the RSC, Sarah wrote what was effectively a 'context-specific' play, making the most of all the special circumstances of its production. We are grateful to all the original performers in that work-in-progress version for their help in shaping the final product, which is also performed by a mix of Cardboard Citizens' actors and conventionally trained actors.

Adrian Jackson, February 2006

About Cardboard Citizens

Cardboard Citizens is a theatre company working particularly with homeless and ex-homeless people, asylum seekers and refugees, as performers, creators, participants and audiences, and producing theatre which derives from or relates to that constituency's experiences. It also produces a number of other related activities, including workshops, training and residencies. The company collaborates with a range of social and arts organisations to deliver its work – this production of VISIBLE is the result of a partnership with the Royal Shakespeare Company, which led to the commissioning of this play and its first performances as work in progress at the RSC's New Work Festival, by a company drawn equally from Cardboard Citizens and the RSC.

CURRENT ACTIVITIES INCLUDE:

Engagement Programme A Forum Theatre tour to hostels and days centres in London. The project, supported by short-term mentoring by the actors, aims to engage homeless people with education, training and support services. The project is delivered in partnership with organisations from the social sector. The most recent piece was Fractured, written by Penny Cliff and Terry O'Leary.

Larger Scale Work A series of productions working on larger scale and in collaboration with other more mainstream arts companies; these have included *The Lower Depths* with London Bubble, *The Beggars Opera* with ENO, and *Pericles* with RSC. In October 2006, the company will present a version of *Timon of Athens* at Stratford as part of the RSC's Complete Works Festival.

Participatory Arts An extensive multi-art form programme of participatory arts activities for homeless and ex-homeless people often delivered in collaboration with other arts organisations

Peer Forum Theatre Forum Theatre productions produced by, with and for a particular community of interest, addressing issues that its constituents face, engendering discussion and debate and enabling solutions to be found. This work has recently been undertaken in the boroughs of Camden (with mental health service users) and Merton (with young people excluded from school).

Regional Development A programme of action research projects in the North West designed to assess the potential for the company to replicate its work outside London. Recent projects have been delivered with young people in Manchester and homeless people in Liverpool.

Training An annual programme of training courses focussing on the techniques of Forum Theatre and the Rainbow of Desires, and delivered by the company's Artistic Director, Adrian Jackson, and Augusto Boal (the inventor of the Theatre of the Oppressed). These courses are supplemented by training commissioned by other organisations both in the UK and overseas; recent overseas training has been delivered in Slovenia, Austria and Spain.

Key Statistics

- Cardboard Citizens works with over 3,000 homeless people a year.

- The company runs over 450 workshops with homeless people a year.

- Each year we enable over 200 homeless people to engage with formal education, training and support services.

- Each week over 250 homeless people access our participatory arts workshops.

- Each year we provide over 400 weeks of paid employment to homeless people as actors.

Forthcoming productions:

IN OCTOBER 2006, CARDBOARD CITIZENS present

Timon of Athens
by William Shakespeare
re-worked by Sarah Woods and Adrian Jackson

Commissioned for the RSC Complete Works Festival 2006
At The Shakespeare Centre in Stratford

Cardboard Citizens renew their relationship with the RSC with their site-specific interpretation of *Timon of Athens*.

> *Who can speak broader than he that has no house to put his head in?*
> *Such may rant against great buildings...   (Timon, Act 2: Scene 1)*

In a world where goals and self-presentation are paramount, where personal trainers and life-coaches help us go about resolving our work-life balance, where the corporation cares, and Shakespeare is used to motivate business people, Cardboard Citizens present a version of *Timon of Athens*.

Timon, a wealthy patron of the arts surrounded by friends and admirers, journeys with terrible inevitability from philanthropy to misanthropy – his money, friends, and mind, all lost along the way.

Following the highly successful co-production of Pericles (2003), this site-specific interpretation of *Timon of Athens*, set in an environment resembling a management seminar, will be staged as part of the RSC's Complete Works Festival, in October 2006.

As with Pericles the text will be pared down, other texts interpellated and the company drawn from Cardboard Citizens' pool of performers with experience of homelessness, and other professional actors, directed by Adrian Jackson, and designed by Fred Meller, with dramaturgy by Sarah Woods.

'It treats the audience to such tempestuous images both Shakespearean and modern day – that they burn indelibly onto the brain and heart' *The Evening Standard on Pericles*

'It has the buzz of a true theatrical event – and its passion cannot be doubted' *The Times*

'The shifts between Shakespeare's drama and the parallel predicaments of contemporary refugees have a piercing dignity and never feel forced or pious' *The Independent*

Further information:

Roy Luxford
royluxford@hotmail.com
tel: +44 (0) 7788 441 634

UK TOUR 2006

Thur 16 – Sat 18 March
www.contact-theatre.org

MANCHESTER Contact Theatre
0161 274 0600

Thur 23 & Fri 24 March
www.trinitytheatre.net

TUNBRIDGE WELLS Trinity Theatre
01892 678 678

Mon 27 & Tue 28 March
www.lighthousepoole.co.uk

POOLE Lighthouse Studio
08700 668 701

Wed 29 & Thur 30 March
www.gardnerarts.co.uk

BRIGHTON Gardner Arts
01273 685861

Fri 31 March & Sat 1 April
www.theatreroyal.org.uk

BATH Ustinov Studio
01225 448844

Tue 4 – Sat 8 April
www.everymanplayhouse.com

LIVERPOOL Everyman
0151 709 4776

Tue 25 April – Sat 6 May
www.sohotheatre.com

LONDON Soho Theatre
0870 429 6883

Sarah Woods
VISIBLE

OBERON BOOKS
LONDON

First published in 2006 by Oberon Books Ltd
521 Caledonian Road, London N7 9RH
Tel: 020 7607 3637 / Fax: 020 7607 3629
e-mail: info@oberonbooks.com
www.oberonbooks.com

A catalogue record for this book is available from the British
Library.

ISBN: 1 84002 665 0

Front cover design: Greg Jakobek at Warsaw

Printed in Great Britain by Antony Rowe Ltd, Chippenham.

CHARACTERS

HATTIE
thirties

ROB
late thirties/early forties – Hattie's husband

ALEX
forties – their neighbour

STUART WHITE
thirties/forties – their friend

CATHERINE
thirties/forties – their neighbour

PETER TILSON
forties – a security guard

Other parts are played by the company.

The play takes place one Sunday.

A forward slash mark / is used to indicate where characters speak at the same time as one another. This usually applies to immediately consecutive speeches unless otherwise stated in the stage directions.

Due to the nature of the piece, some elements of the dialogue will change with each performance. Guides to these appear in italics and square brackets within the speeches.

ACT ONE

SCENE ONE

The kitchen in ROB and HATTIE's house. There is a big table and a kitchen surface on which there stands a large joint of beef – which remains there throughout the play – and various other ingredients, including a bag of dates with their stones in. Most surfaces are covered. Shouting from off-stage.

ROB: (*Off.*) So it's my fault now, is it?

HATTIE: (*Off.*) It's your fault you left the door open. You know he goes in there.

ROB: (*Off.*) And how did he get into the house in the first place? Who let him into the house?

HATTIE: (*Off.*) He comes in through the windows.

ROB: (*Off.*) Who opened the windows?

HATTIE: (*Off.*) I have to air the house.

ROB: (*Off.*) And I have to walk in and out of rooms.

HATTIE: (*Off.*) You can shut the doors behind you.

ROB: (*Off.*) He walks round here like he owns the place.

He storms onto the stage – looking under things and opening cupboards.

Whose house is this? It's my house. I decide who comes in and who doesn't.

HATTIE enters with a pile of sheets on top of which is part of a dead bird.

HATTIE: He won't be in here, will he?

ROB: How do you know?

HATTIE: Because all these doors were shut.

ROB: Rasputin?

HATTIE: Because I shut them.

ROB sneezes near the joint of meat as HATTIE closes doors after him.

Will you not sneeze on the beef?

ROB: It's the cat. That's why we don't own one.

HATTIE: It's not just the sneezing, is it?

ROB: Because I can't have one in the house.

HATTIE: You hate animals.

ROB: It's an allergy.

HATTIE: You don't like people much –

ROB: It's an allergic reaction.

HATTIE: But animals –

He continues looking for the cat throughout the scene – taking out his rage about what HATTIE's saying on the absent cat.

ROB: Razzy!

HATTIE: If you can't bring yourself to have any feelings for your own wife, it's hardly surprising you're not an animal-lover.

ROB: Where is he? Where is he?

HATTIE: It's not like you don't have any feelings for modern art or Asian food –

ROB sneezes.

ROB: I like Asian food –

HATTIE: (*Shouts.*) I know you like Asian food! And even if you don't, it doesn't matter. It's me! Your wife!

ROB: I do have feelings for you.

HATTIE: No you don't!

ROB: I just don't show them.

HATTIE: That's no good to me, is it? It's like telling me my birthday presents are in the attic and never getting them down.

He sneezes twice.

ROB: Rasputin?

HATTIE: Perhaps they are – perhaps all the presents you've never bought me for all my birthdays and Christmases and Anniversaries and Valentines and Easter / are up –

ROB: I didn't know I had to do Easter –

18

HATTIE: Up there in the attic, all wrapped up in a huge parcel with a great big bow.

She follows him around as he looks in cupboards.

If I don't know they're there, why should I believe they exist.

ROB: Do you believe there are people in some parts of the world who don't have enough to eat and who don't have clean water or adequate medical provision?

HATTIE: Of course I do.

ROB: But you haven't seen them.

HATTIE: I've seen them on the TV.

ROB: Not all of them.

HATTIE: I've seen their representatives.

ROB: You haven't really seen them. But still you choose to believe in them. And yet you refuse to believe that I love you –

He looks in another cupboard.

Here, puss –

HATTIE: I can see you.

ROB: You can't see my feelings.

HATTIE: Don't you think I should be able to feel them?

They look at each other for a moment, a couple in crisis.

ROB: Bloody cat thinks it can come round here whenever it likes and leave corpses on our bed.

HATTIE: I can feel the feelings of the starving people when I see them on TV.

ROB does a huge series of sneezes – maybe five.

Why do you always sneeze when we're arguing?

He sneezes again, once.

Perhaps it's me you're allergic to.

ROB: Perhaps it's your feelings.

HATTIE: What did you say?

HATTIE and ROB look at each other for a moment. Before ROB can reply, there is a whistling sound – like a dove cooing – from

19

the back door. HATTIE looks alarmed – she glances at ROB – has he heard? ROB is listening. The cooing stops.

ROB: What was that?

HATTIE: What?

ROB: That noise.

The cooing sounds again.

There.

HATTIE: I can't hear anything.

HATTIE is frozen. We hear ALEX from the other side of the back door.

ALEX: (*Furtive, off.*) Hattie? Hattie –

ALEX opens the door a little and peeps in.

HATTIE: (*Too jolly.*) Alex –

ALEX: Hattie –

He sees ROB.

Rob.

ROB isn't suspicious.

ROB: Alex.

ALEX and HATTIE look at each other.

ALEX: Hi. How are things?

ROB: Not bad.

HATTIE: Fine.

ROB: Did you hear that noise?

ALEX: What noise?

ROB: That bird noise.

ALEX: No.

ROB: We've got a bit of a cat problem.

HATTIE: Would you get the Le Creuset out, Rob?

ROB sneezes.

ROB: We're working to a strict timetable, Alex.

ALEX: I can see.

ROB goes off to get the Le Creuset as ALEX moves to stand very close to HATTIE.

HATTIE: What did you do that for?

ALEX: I didn't know he was here. I thought he was at the gym.

HATTIE: His car's out the front.

ALEX: I came round the back. I had to see you. I couldn't wait –

ROB sneezes as he comes back in. HATTIE quickly gives ALEX the bag of dates which is sitting on the side.

HATTIE: Here you go. Twelve-thirty for one.

ALEX: Hattie –

HATTIE: Where's the Le Creuset?

ROB: I don't know.

HATTIE: Where did you look?

ROB: Under the stairs.

HATTIE: It's on top of the wardrobe in the spare room.

ROB: Right. Are those our dates?

ALEX and HATTIE look at them. A beat – how to get out of this one? No matter how suspiciously HATTIE and ALEX behave, and no matter how worried they are about being found out, ROB never gets suspicious.

ALEX: Yes.

HATTIE: Yes.

ROB: We need them for the Sticky Toffee Pudding.

HATTIE: Alex said he'd do the Sticky Toffee Pudding.

ALEX: Me?

ROB: Really?

HATTIE: He said he'd like to.

ALEX: I'd like to.

HATTIE: He'd like to.

ALEX: You've got enough on your plate.

They all laugh a little – HATTIE and ALEX slightly too much.

HATTIE: Enough on our plate!

ROB: Very kind of you.

ROB starts to collect things from round the kitchen to show ALEX.

Have you got Camp Coffee?

ALEX: I'm sorry?

ALEX brings the Camp Coffee over.

ROB: Contrary to popular belief, they didn't stop making it in nineteen-fifty-five. You can still get it in the supermarket.

He gives it to ALEX.

I'm presuming you haven't got any?

ALEX: I don't know.

HATTIE: Rob does puddings.

ALEX: I don't go in the kitchen much.

ROB: Four ounces of butter, six ounces of soft brown sugar creamed.

ALEX: (*To HATTIE.*) Hattie –

HATTIE: Sugar –

ROB gives ALEX the soft brown sugar and goes off round the kitchen again.

ROB: That's important. Add four beaten eggs –

ALEX: (*To HATTIE.*) Hattie –

HATTIE: Four eggs.

ALEX: (*To HATTIE.*) I'm doing this for you, Hattie.

HATTIE: Beaten.

ALEX: (*To HATTIE.*) This pudding.

ROB: Bit at a time.

ALEX: (*To HATTIE.*) This Sticky Toffee Pudding.

ROB: Then eight ounces of flour, sieved with a teaspoon of bicarbonate of soda.

ROB returns and gives him a packet of bicarbonate of soda.

ALEX: Bicarb.

HATTIE: Bicarbonate of soda.

ALEX: Did you hear me?

ROB: Add eight ounces of chopped dates –

HATTIE: He's got the dates.

ROB: Two teaspoons of Camp Coffee.

HATTIE: You'll have to chop them.

ALEX: (*To HATTIE.*) I'd do anything for you.

HATTIE looks at the date packet.

ROB: Half a pint of boiling water –

HATTIE: And take the stones out.

ALEX: (*To HATTIE.*) I love you –

ROB: It sounds awful, but actually it works.

HATTIE: These have got stones in.

ALEX: Hattie –

ROB: It looks like pancake batter.

HATTIE: He's bought the wrong ones.

ALEX: Hattie –

ROB: Cake tin, in the oven for an hour.

ALEX: Tell me you feel the same.

ROB: So working backwards –

HATTIE: Lunch is half-twelve for one.

ROB: You need to get it in the oven by eleven.

HATTIE: It's ten-thirty now.

HATTIE looks desperately at ALEX. ALEX is loaded up with ingredients.

ROB: You'd better get cracking –

She manoeuvres ALEX to the door.

ALEX: Hattie –

HATTIE: I'll open the door.

ALEX: Hattie –

HATTIE: Goodbye, Alex.

ROB: Thanks, Alex.

ALEX goes. ROB indicates the bird remains on the laundry which HATTIE is still holding.

This thing stinks.

HATTIE: I'm going to clean it up.

ROB exits. A moment. The cooing sound from the back door.

No!

She listens for ROB to really go. She waits and waits – finally ALEX cooes again.

No –

They wait. Finally, HATTIE opens the back door. ALEX enters, still with the ingredients. HATTIE is already clearing up the bird remains.

ALEX: Hattie.

HATTIE: I can't do this now, Alex.

She drops the bird remains into the bin.

ALEX: Hattie.

ALEX carries around all the ingredients he's holding.

I want to say – I'm sorry about Friday.

HATTIE starts to take the full bin liner out of the bin.

I had to go back to the office.

HATTIE: What for?

ALEX taps his nose.

ALEX: GCHQ. Official secrets act. Please don't punish me.

HATTIE: I'm not.

ALEX: I'd never have left you sitting there if I could help it.

HATTIE: It's fine.

HATTIE ties up the full bin liner.

ALEX: I've missed you so much.

So much has happened and I want to tell you about it so much. Philippa and I had a huge row when I got back.

She turns round with the bin liner and comes face to face with ALEX.

HATTIE: If I don't concentrate on lunch, I don't think I can cope.

He moves towards her.

Don't.

HATTIE heads out of the back door with the bin liner as they continue, ALEX follows.

Rob'll be back in a minute – he's only gone to the spare room for the Le Creuset.

ALEX: I've spent all the time we've been apart imagining you and now I'm looking at you I feel like I'm drowning in your face.

ROB sneezes and enters, with the Le Creuset. It is very big and heavy and he staggers about, looking for somewhere to put it down.

ROB: Hattie. Hattie?

No reply. There's no room on any of the surfaces, so he dumps it on the laundry on the kitchen table. There is the muffled sound of a cat dying. ROB looks at the pile. He tries to look under the Le Creuset without moving it.

(*Soft.*) Razzy?

He looks more closely. He sneezes.

Rasputin?

He lifts off the Le Creuset and there in the sheets, now dead, is Rasputin.

No.

ROB picks Rasputin out from the sheets. He sneezes. We hear ALEX and HATTIE coming back.

HATTIE: I've got to think about the vegetables. If I don't get them on at the right time, the dinner won't work.

ROB looks round for somewhere to put the cat. He sneezes again. He puts it behind one of the cushions on the sofa, picks up the Le Creuset and exits as ALEX and HATTIE enter. They speak very quietly and secretly and urgently.

Please don't.

ALEX: You feel the same.

HATTIE: We're in my kitchen.

ALEX: I love you wherever we are.

HATTIE gets vegetables out as ALEX puts the pudding ingredients down. First sprouts in an opended net, which she gives to ALEX. Then carrots and parsnips, which she keeps hold of.

HATTIE: I've got five people for Sunday lunch in a hundred and twenty minutes.

ALEX: Let me hold you.

HATTIE sets off across the room away from him – he pursues her.

HATTIE: And my husband and your wife are two of them.

She looks at the vegetables in her hands.

What am I doing?

ALEX: They're carrots. And the white ones are parsnips.

HATTIE: I've got to peel them, Alex.

ALEX: Let me peel them with you.

They peel vegetables.

HATTIE: You've got to make the Sticky Toffee Pudding.

ALEX: I know that. I know that.

They can hardly resist the pull of each other, their words are like a sonnet, communicating the things they can't express.

HATTIE: I can't find the sprouts.

ALEX: They're here.

He holds them up.

Phil's having a lie down.

HATTIE: Is she?

The ACTOR PLAYING ALEX has forgotten his next line. The ACTOR PLAYING HATTIE waits, and then:

Alex –

Still nothing – so she feeds him a line with the prompt word 'want' in it.

You know what I want.

ALEX gets back on track – but goes back to an earlier line.

ALEX: Let me peel them with you.

HATTIE: You've got to make the Sticky Toffee Pudding.

ALEX: I know that.

HATTIE: I can't find the sprouts.

ALEX: They're here.

Phil's having a lie down.

HATTIE: Is she?

ALEX: You want this as much as me.

We hear sneezing off as ROB returns.

HATTIE: Rob –

They both panic.

Quick –

HATTIE shoves ALEX into a tall cupboard – he's still holding the sprouts. ROB enters with the Le Creuset. He is in a state. HATTIE has returned to preparing the vegetables.

You found it, then?

ROB: Yes.

Once again, he looks for somewhere to put it. HATTIE makes a space and he puts it down. ROB sees all the Sticky Toffee Pudding ingredients.

HATTIE: I'm preparing the carrots.

She peels and chops the winter vegetables.

ROB: Alex brought the dates back.

HATTIE: They had some already.

ROB: And Camp Coffee?

HATTIE: Apparently.

ROB sneezes.

Did you find him?

ROB: (*Guilty.*) What?

HATTIE: Rasputin.

ROB: No.

ROB starts to put things away. HATTIE, worried that he'll find ALEX, is taking them off him. ROB, worried HATTIE might find Rasputin wants to keep her away from the sofa – there are longish silences between lines.

Did you?

HATTIE: (*Guilty.*) No.

ROB: He must have got out again.

Hattie –

He looks at her. He gets ready to tell her about the cat.

HATTIE: What?

He is about to tell her. ALEX's mobile phone goes off in the cupboard. HATTIE and ROB both listen to it – ROB quizzically, HATTIE with increasing horror.

That's your mobile.

ROB: Flight of the Valkyries?

HATTIE: I changed the tune.

ROB pats his pocket.

It's in your coat.

In the hallway.

ROB goes to get it. The phone stops ringing. HATTIE opens the cupboard. ALEX is inside, on his mobile, still juggling the sprouts.

ALEX: (*On the phone.*) Any minute. Just a minute.

'Bye.

He hangs up.

HATTIE: What are you doing?

ALEX comes out of the cupboard.

ALEX: That was Philippa. She's woken up. I've got to go home.

ROB comes back on, bumping into ALEX and sending him into HATTIE – he drops some sprouts. They spring apart.

ROB: Sorry!

HATTIE: Sorry.

ROB registers ALEX.

ROB: Alex –

They all pick up the sprouts and give them back to ALEX.

ALEX: Sorry.

ROB: Sorry about that.

ROB looks at ALEX holding the sprouts.

HATTIE: Just peel them, cut the bottoms and I'll do the rest.

Twelve-thirty for one.

ROB: What?

HATTIE: Alex popped round for the sprouts.

ROB: Sprouts?

ALEX: Sprouts?

HATTIE: He's taking the sprouts. To prepare. I'm running very late.

ROB: What about the Sticky Toffee Pudding?

HATTIE: He says it's all under control.

ROB: Fancy you having Camp Coffee!

ALEX: Hattie –

HATTIE: Did you find the phone?

ROB: It had stopped ringing.

ALEX: I'd better –

He signals going.

ROB: Don't go on my account.

ALEX: No, no – of course not, no – never. No.

HATTIE: No!

She laughs, ALEX and ROB join in. A moment. The land line rings.

ROB: 'Phone.

HATTIE: I'll get it.

We listen as HATTIE answers the phone.

Hello?

Catherine.

ROB: Sunday lunch.

ALEX: Yeah.

HATTIE: Oh.

ROB: How long is it since we last had dinner together?

HATTIE: Oh dear.

ALEX: Is it a year?

ROB: Could be.

HATTIE: Don't worry. I'm sure he's somewhere.

ROB: Were you at ours last New Year?

ALEX: No. We were at home.

ROB: Course you were.

HATTIE: Of course. I'll have a look. And Rob will. And Alex is here. I'll tell him.

Okay?

You're all right.

'Bye.

HATTIE puts the phone down.

It was Catherine. She can't find Rasputin.

ROB: Rasputin?

HATTIE: He hasn't come home for his breakfast.

ROB looks very worried.

I said I'd tell you Alex.

ALEX: Good.

HATTIE: Have you seen him?

ROB: No.

He looks half-heartedly under the table, calling the cat.

Rasputin –

He sneezes.

HATTIE: He's round here all the time.

ROB: Here puss, puss…

HATTIE: Sleeps on our bed.

ROB: Here puss, puss –

The ACTOR PLAYING ALEX has the urge to laugh – partly at the ACTOR PLAYING ROB but partly out of nervousness. He turns away for a moment.

HATTIE: Rob doesn't like him.

ROB: It's not that I don't like him. Rasputin!

ROB sneezes five or more times in a row. The ACTOR PLAYING ALEX wants to laugh again. He tries to hide his face. The ACTOR PLAYING ROB is getting pissed off with him.

HATTIE: He hates cats.

ROB: I don't hate him.

He continues looking.

HATTIE: And above all he hates Rasputin.

ROB: I don't hate him at all.

The ACTOR PLAYING ALEX starts to deliver his next line, but starts laughing again.

THE ACTOR PLAYING ALEX: Do you like Buster?

The ACTORS playing HATTIE and ROB are getting worried.

HATTIE: He likes dogs.

ROB: Rasputin uses our garden as a big litter tray, that's all I said.

HATTIE: You said you wanted Rasputin dead –

ROB: (*Shouts.*) I don't want Rasputin dead! I never said I want Rasputin dead!

ROB sneezes once.

I never said that!

It's ALEX's line. ALEX is lost and goes back to his previous line.

THE ACTOR PLAYING ALEX: Do you like Buster?

HATTIE: He likes dogs.

ROB: Rasputin uses our garden as a big litter tray, that's all I said.

HATTIE: You said you wanted Rasputin dead –

ROB: (*Shouts.*) I don't want Rasputin dead! I never said I want Rasputin dead!

ROB sneezes once.

I never said that!

The ACTOR PLAYING ALEX starts to laugh again. He tries to stop himself – this time it's harder, he's losing it.

THE ACTOR PLAYING ROB: I never said I want Rasputin dead!

ROB sneezes once.

I never said that!

The ACTOR PLAYING ALEX shakes his head. He can't continue. He's dropping a few sprouts which the ACTOR PLAYING ROB might kick out of the way. The ACTOR PLAYING ROB tries again.

(*As ROB.*) I didn't mean I wanted him dead. I just meant –

ALEX: I've heard you –

　To HATTIE.

I've heard him say he wants him dead!

HATTIE: He's heard you.

ALEX: I didn't mean I wanted him dead.

　The ACTOR PLAYING ALEX has said one of ROB's lines.

THE ACTOR PLAYING ROB: (*As ROB.*) I didn't mean I wanted him dead. I just meant –

　The ACTOR PLAYING ALEX is meant to interrupt, but doesn't. A long pause. We see him visibly realise – he's not really acting anymore.

THE ACTOR PLAYING ALEX: What?

THE ACTOR PLAYING HATTIE: (*As HATTIE.*) What?

ROB: I don't see why I should spend my life cleaning up after someone else's filthy cat in my own home and be happy about it. I should go and tell Catherine, nice as she is, that she's spoilt her cat so much she's turned it into a monster and, as much as I like her as a neighbour, Rasputin is completely out of control and should not be allowed to behave the way he does in other people's homes and gardens – especially when I've put a lot of time and money into our garden and hers is a perfect cat litter tray.

　The ACTOR PLAYING ALEX does not give the line he should. Eventually:

THE ACTOR PLAYING ALEX: I don't think I can do this anymore.

THE ACTOR PLAYING HATTIE: You're fine.

THE ACTOR PLAYING ALEX: It's all shit. I've finished.

THE ACTOR PLAYING ROB: Alex –

THE ACTOR PLAYING ALEX: My name's [*insert real name of ACTOR PLAYING ALEX*].

THE ACTOR PLAYING ROB: [*Real name of ACTOR PLAYING ALEX.*]

　The ACTOR PLAYING ALEX starts to walk off, then turns back and returns, still holding the sprouts.

THE ACTOR PLAYING ALEX: I'm sorry. Just got a bit too much for me.

He launches back into the script, going back a bit.

I've heard you –

To HATTIE.

I've heard him say he wants him dead!

HATTIE: He's heard you.

ROB: I didn't mean I wanted him dead. I just meant –

THE ACTOR PLAYING ALEX: What happened was –
I was in Massachusetts, and I met this American guy who invited me round to his friend's that evening for dinner.

When he came to pick me up, it started to snow really, really heavily and the journey – which should have taken half an hour – took nearly four. There was points where we was having to get out of the car and bounce it on the road to get it to move. There was people you could see stranded – it was like really hairy. And we daren't stop – once we got momentum. You knew if you stop, you might not ever move again.

When we finally arrive at the apartment block, we knock on the door, make plenty of noise – can't get any answer. So we go back out to the car park and we're going to drive back to where we'd set off from. But the car had disappeared. The car park was just flat with snow. And you know the car was under there somewhere, but it was like: where?

So we decide to persuade the janitor to let us in with the pass key. We find him, but he won't let us in because he's never seen us before. I've met plenty of other people who'd go: come and stay with us, but he wasn't that type, to go out of his way to help you.

So now we're stuck, standing outside the apartment with nowhere to go. And I decide to kick the door off. Because I've done it a few times before, getting in squats. It was a nice, narrow passageway, and as long as I get enough purchase and there's a bit of pressure on the door, I could ping it off – the lock'll give way and it'll ping open. And all you have to do is screw the thing back together again.

So I get my back up against the wall and start pushing against the door.

The ACTOR PLAYING ROB marches him to the edge of the stage, to talk to him privately – we can hear bits of their hushed conversation.

THE ACTOR PLAYING ROB: Just do the script.

THE ACTOR PLAYING ALEX: Don't shout at me.

THE ACTOR PLAYING ROB: I'm not shouting.

THE ACTOR PLAYING ALEX: Or I'll fuck off.

THE ACTOR PLAYING ROB: You're not going to fuck off – no one's going to fuck off.

They re-enter.

THE ACTOR PLAYING ALEX: I've just got to get my head straight for a moment.

(*As ALEX.*) I've heard you –

(*To HATTIE.*) I've heard him say he wants him dead!

HATTIE: He's heard you.

ALEX: What?

ROB: I don't see why I should spend my life cleaning up after someone else's filthy cat in my own home, when Catherine's turned it into a monster – and I've put a lot of time and money into our garden and hers is a perfect cat litter tray.

ALEX: He's got a point.

The doorbell rings.

ROB: I'll go.

ROB exits. At first we think the ACTOR PLAYING ALEX is on script – but no – he's reverted to his story – which he has started again.

ALEX: So I'm back up against the wall, putting lots and lots of pressure on the door, and instead of it pinging open, the door, the frame and parts of the wall crashed down and there was this – just – it was like a cave now, it looked like a cave. And the noise it made – it was like a bomb going off.

So we get in the flat and we pick up the door and prop it up against the hole in the wall I've just created. Switch on the television and make some coffee.

The ACTOR PLAYING HATTIE watches, looking utterly stuck. The ACTOR PLAYING ROB watches from the wings. Maybe the STAGE MANAGER too. HATTIE watches and watches – we think she might cry.

And we start seeing news bulletins on the television about the snow. They've declared a state of emergency because there's been eleven foot snow drifts. And when they're declaring a state of emergency, you know you're in trouble.

After about an hour, the American guy decides to give me a guided tour of the apartment. When we get to the second bedroom, we looked in and there's a body on the bed.

HATTIE exits. The ACTOR PLAYING ALEX just sits. For quite a while. Then we hear a mobile phone ringing and someone answering it off stage. And then nothing again. Then the ACTOR PLAYING ROB comes on. He sits on the sofa with the ACTOR PLAYING ALEX, but doesn't engage with him. The STAGE MANAGER and the ACTOR PLAYING HATTIE watch from the wings. The STAGE MANAGER comes on a few steps.

THE ACTOR PLAYING ROB: (*Quiet.*) Come with me.

He puts his hand out to take the ACTOR PLAYING ALEX's arm. The ACTOR PLAYING ALEX pulls away from him violently.

THE ACTOR PLAYING ALEX: Get off!

THE ACTOR PLAYING ROB: All right.

The ACTOR PLAYING ROB gets up and exits the way he came. The ACTOR PLAYING ALEX sits looking pissed off for a little bit longer.

THE ACTOR PLAYING ALEX: Sorry.

He exits through the audience. The stage is left empty.

SCENE TWO

After a while, STUART WHITE the Games Show Host enters with a hand-held mic.

STUART: (*On mic.*) Hello. Hello, hello. Good evening.

Has anyone seen Treacle?

He asks the audience.

Have you seen Treacle?

Has anyone seen Treacle anywhere? Or Honey? What about Sugar?

He looks around – much as ROB did for the cat.

Only they promised me they'd be here tonight.

He does a funny dance for a moment.

They promised me. They promised me they'd help out with tonight's problems and puzzles.

He starts to clap his hands above his head: two claps and then waits for two.

Come on.

He gets the audience doing it.

Can you do that?

He keeps clapping.

Clap – clap –

He waits for two counts.

Clap – clap –

He waits for two counts.

Hands above your head.

He stops clapping.

Now can you do this: Trea-cle.

He waits for two beats.

Ho-ney!

He waits for two beats.

Su-gar!

He waits for two beats.

Let's put the two together. Treacle!

He claps for two claps. Then this calling and clapping is repeated until the audience have built up a rhythm. Once the audience are clapping and calling, STUART speaks into his microphone as he starts to make his way off stage.

Where's Treacle? Treacle?

As STUART exits, the lights go down and sparkly coloured lights scan the stage and auditorium. There's dry ice and music with sung and whispered voices.

PRE-RECORDED: Treacle (Treacle, Treacle) –

Honey (Honey, Honey) –

Sugar (Sugar, Sugar) –

Where's Treacle?

Where's Honey?

Where's Sugar?

Then big, building, joyful music as we build to the entrance of TREACLE and HONEY and SUGAR.

STUART: Ladies and gentlemen – please welcome on stage: Treacle and Honey and Sugar –

The stage fills with bright and colourful light and the music is ecstatic and anthemic as TREACLE and HONEY and SUGAR enter. STUART enters after them and they move into a song and dance routine – everyone's having a great time. STUART sings with them and interjects with comments to the audience. The words of the song are displayed on the video screen with a ball that bounces across the words. The audience are encouraged to join in.

ANIMALS: (*Sing.*) If the world is a spanner
That's got in your works,
If you're all broken down
And feeling terribly hurt.

HONEY: (*Speaks.*) Don't feel isolated
You're not on your own

SUGAR: (*Speaks.*) When Treacle and Sugar
And Honey are home.

TREACLE: (*Speaks.*) Hop over to our place
Knock on the door –

HONEY: (*Speaks.*) We'll show you it's simpler
Than you've ever thought.

ANIMALS: (*Sing.*) Oooh-oooh-oooh-oooh!
Life is sweet – it's Honey.
Sticky and sweet – it's Treacle.

37

Sugar and Treacle and Honey –
Get yourself a big spoon.
When you're getting the jitters,
Think of yourself –
Don't fret about others,
It's bad for your health.

HONEY: (*Speaks.*) Feel good you've got money
And comfort and warmth,

SUGAR: (*Speaks.*) That your only food crisis
Is you can't eat it all.

TREACLE: (*Speaks.*) You were born lucky –
It's nothing you've done,

SUGAR: (*Speaks.*) Stop flagellating,
Gyrate and have fun!

ANIMALS: (*Sing.*) Oooh-oooh-oooh-oooh!
Life is sweet – it's Honey.
Sticky and sweet – it's Treacle.
Sugar and Treacle and Honey –
Get yourself a big spoon.
Life is sweet – it's Honey.
Sticky and sweet – it's Treacle.
Sugar and Treacle and Honey –
Get yourself a big –
Get yourself a big –
Get yourself a big –
…Spoon!

STUART: Good evening, good evening, good people – and
welcome to:

Problems – puzzles…

*He invites to audience to join in his catch phrase – he and the
animals do thumbs down/thumbs up/thumbs up/thumbs down
hand gesture.*

Puzzles – problems.

We've got no idea how things are going to turn out tonight,
but there are three things I can guarantee you:

TREACLE and HONEY and SUGAR mime to this next bit.

There'll be problems.

They hold their heads in their hands.

We'll be puzzled.

They shake their heads around between their hands.

And there'll be prizes!

They go crazy.

So – who's going to play? Who's going to play with us tonight?

STUART moves into the audience with his microphone, to find people. The furry animals can help – they also need to set up two sets of two high stools for the contestants.

Which lucky people are going to play Problems – Puzzles, Puzzles – Problems?

He gets contestants from the audience: it doesn't matter what order they come in. One of them is the PLANT ACTOR. They are sent onto the stage, where they are greeted and seated by TREACLE, HONEY or SUGAR – who shake their hands or cuddle them. The animals are always very friendly and cuddly. They put badges on them: TREACLE'S TEAM and HONEY'S TEAM. When all four contestants are assembled – two to a team with at least one man on TREACLE's Team, and the PLANT ACTOR and someone else on HONEY's, STUART returns to the stage. During this next section additional banter can be improvised where needed.

Let's hear it for our lovely contestants!

He introduces the first contestant.

Contestant number one – what's your name?

CONTESTANT ONE: I'm [*CONTESTANT ONE's name*].

STUART: And where are you from, [*CONTESTANT ONE's name*]?

CONTESTANT ONE: [*CONTESTANT ONE's home town.*]

STUART: (*A bit more banter then on to CONTESTANT TWO.*)
　　　Contestant number two: what's your name?

CONTESTANT TWO: I'm [*CONTESTANT TWO's name*].

STUART: And where are you from, [*CONTESTANT TWO's name*]?

CONTESTANT TWO: [*CONTESTANT TWO's home town.*]

STUART: Ladies and gentlemen, we're in for a treat tonight, because it says here that in your spare time you can't stop tap dancing.

Music plays – they get the audience to clap and CONTESTANT TWO to tap dance – STUART and the animals dance too.

Contestant number three. What's your name and where are you from?

CONTESTANT THREE: I'm [*CONTESTANT THREE's name and home town*].

STUART: Tell me, [*CONTESTANT THREE's name*], if you could be an edible item, what edible item would you be?

CONTESTANT THREE: I'd be a [*names foodstuff*].

STUART can improvise around: You can choose anything. It's in our imaginations, it's not really happening.

STUART: I think I'd be a – no – no – I have absolutely no desire to be a foodstuff. You might have some weird compulsion, some terrible obsession with [*name of CONTESTANT THREE's foodstuff*], not me. No.

The PLANT ACTOR is CONTESTANT FOUR.

Contestant number four, what's your name?

PLANT ACTOR: Bola.

STUART: What's your surname? Cks?

She shakes her head.

And it says here you've just been on holiday?

PLANT ACTOR: No.

STUART: One of your friends who I think is here tonight –

PLANT ACTOR: No –

STUART: Has told us you've just returned from a lovely holiday in the Caribbean.

And here's a picture of you on your holiday –

And he shows a picture of a severed pig's head wearing sunglasses. And she doesn't look happy about it.

PLANT ACTOR: I think that's a bit offensive.

STUART: To who? You or the pig?

She shakes her head in disbelief.

You don't have to worry about offending me.

SUGAR comes and gives STUART a big hug. STUART tries to extricate himself.

All right, Sugar.

(*To the audience.*) Never let one of these into bed with you, eh? Bestiality – not interesting. We're different species – let's stay that way.

Ladies and Gentlemen, it's time to play:

He encourages them to join in with the gesture and shouting the name of the show, as do TREACLE and HONEY.

Problems – Puzzles, Puzzles – Problems.

Musical sting and we're into the games. A furry animal stands with each team – SUGAR stands in the middle.

Right, time for our first round: Problems and Objections. A game you are familiar with.

In this round, I will set the two teams one problem, and they have to make a choice between two options, to rectify that particular problem. And there is a right answer.

Here's the first one: Life is a Beach.

HONEY and SUGAR walk along the 'beach'.

You are walking along a beach with your loved one. A few other people are strolling nearby. Suddenly, a large wave comes in and sweeps your loved one and another person out to sea.

HONEY and TREACLE are the two people – swept to either side of the stage. HONEY is the Loved One, TREACLE is the Stranger – they both have their identities written on cards. They hold up the cards and mime drowning and waving – as SUGAR panics on the 'beach'.

Both appear to be drowning. There we are look. There's your loved one. There's your stranger. Although you are a strong swimmer, it is clear that you will not be able to save both of them. What is the right thing to do?

Honey and Treacle drowning away there.

Who are you going to save? For fifty points. Timer, please.

Music as they work it out, STUART reiterates things and SUGAR paces the 'beach'.

Your loved one. Or the stranger. Who gets the kiss of life? Who gets a watery grave? Who do you walk away across that beach with? You decide.

Music finishes – time up.

Treacle's Team. What have you got?

TREACLE's Team say their answer – bit of banter around it.

Honey's Team.

HONEY's Team say their answer – banter around it.

And the correct answer, for fifty points, is: Save your loved one.

SUGAR saves HONEY who is delighted, while TREACLE – who is not – drowns.

Treacle, you're a goner.

Course it is. Kill someone you don't know. Kill a stranger. Okay? So that's fifty points to [*Honey/Treacle's*] team.

SUGAR is waving and leaving.

Bye-bye, Sugar. Will you come back and help us later?

SUGAR nods and exits, still waving. TREACLE starts to leave, upset.

Are you going too, Treacle? We've upset him – sensitive creatures. They're not like us. Bye-bye.

TREACLE exits.

Okay – next puzzle: Punching in the Street.

Sounds nasty.

HONEY and STUART mime the next one.

You and I are walking along the street when you become angry with me because of something I have said. You punch me maliciously and hard –

HONEY mimes punching him – he mimes reeling backwards.

Here –

He indicates where and she punches him again.

I stagger backwards and, in doing so move out of the way of a body falling from the sky, the presence of which I was not aware – and which would have landed on top of me. Ouch. Was punching me, hard –

She mimes punching him again.

All right! Was it the right thing to do? Start the timer.

Music as they work it out and STUART reiterates things.

Interesting. For fifty points. Was punching me, maliciously and hard, the right thing to do? Was punching me –

HONEY goes to punch him again.

Watch it – was it the right thing to do?

He indicates CONTESTANT THREE.

He's thinking about his [*CONTESTANT THREE's food item from earlier*]. I'm thinking about roast beef and Yorkshire pudding with all the veg. And for pudding – no.

No!

The music finishes – time up.

Time's up. Treacle's Team. What have you got?

TREACLE's Team tell their answer – banter around it.

Honey's Team.

HONEY's Team tell us their answer – banter around it.

And the correct answer, for fifty points, is: Yes, punching me is the right thing to do. Can you believe that? Punching me is the right thing to do. An act of violence is okay if it prevents a greater act of violence. Got that?

HONEY exits.

Where's she gone now?

They're a law unto themselves, those animals. You give them a job description and you know what they say? They can't read it.

And at the end of that round Treacle's Team have got [*correct score*] points. And Honey's team have got [*correct score*] points.

SUGAR comes on, dragging a large cardboard box.

What's going on here?

SUGAR points at the box.

What've you got there?

HONEY enters with another box.

What have you got in these boxes, Honey?

HONEY shows him a contestant.

You're going to put the contestants in the boxes?

STUART gets hold of a contestant.

You want to put a contestant in the box? Will this one do?

HONEY shakes her head. STUART goes to another one.

How about this one?

HONEY shakes her head as TREACLE enters with the final box.

No! Not the contestants. That would be going a bit far, wouldn't it!

The animals try to mime 'people in the boxes'.

Is it a game?

The animals nod and mime that there are illegal migrants in the boxes.

It is. You've got people.

There are people hiding in the boxes.

They're very frightened – look at that.

They don't want to be caught.

SUGAR shows us a passport.

Because they've got no passports. They're seeking asylum!

Okay –

In each of these boxes is a person. The last thing they want is to be caught and deported. So they're going to stay very still.

Everyone on this side of the audience, you're on Honey's team, and if you see one of the boxes move shout out 'Honey!'

He gets them to do it.

Everyone on this side, you're on Treacle's Team. If you see one of the boxes move, shout 'Treacle!'

He gets them to do it.

How many points do they get if they Peek a Seeker?

The animals mime one hundred.

For one hundred points. If you see one of those boxes move,
if you Peek a Seeker – that's a hundred points.

The animals go, waving.

Bye-bye Honey. Bye-bye Sugar. Bye-bye Treacle.

There is a musical sting.

Now we all know what that sound means. It means
someone's trying to get in touch.

He moves the contestants onto the front row.

Come on – come and sit down here so you can see.

As he does so, he looks round for SUGAR.

(*To the audience.*) Sugar? Has anyone seen Sugar?

(*To the contestants.*) There you go. That's it.

(*To the audience.*) Where's that penguin got to?

Someone's got a problem for us to solve tonight.

He waves his hand and the sting sounds again.

We all know what that sound means –

SUGAR enters in a hurry.

Where've you been?

He mimes that he can't find the remote control unit.

You can't find the remote control? Where is it?

SUGAR shakes his head.

You don't know. Doesn't listen to a word.

STUART grabs SUGAR's head.

I mean – where are his ears. Has he even got any?

SUGAR is getting cross – STUART holds his beak shut.

Now – don't get snappy. Anyone speak Penguinese?

*He lets go of him, pushing him away. Speaks to him loudly and
clearly.*

All you have to do is run on, give me the remote control,
give the audience a wave, and run off. Isn't it? That's what
we employ you for.

You want to watch your step. Plenty more penguins in the sea. You'll be out of a job soon. Probably what he wants. Claim some benefits.

SUGAR points to STUART's jacket pocket.

What? There are no tuna steaks in there.

SUGAR manhandles STUART trying to get the remote out of his pocket.

What's it doing in there?

He wallops SUGAR round the head.

You're a waste of fish. Get off.

Can't get the penguins these days, can you?

SUGAR exits.

They come over here, start laying eggs and the next thing you know our schools are full of little penguins with their fish paste sandwiches.

STUART presses a button on the remote and the video link comes on. On the screen is LILLIAN, an old woman, on the street.

It's Lillian. Lillian from High Wycombe. What's the problem, Lillian!

LILLIAN: Is this live?

STUART: It is love.

LILLIAN: Hello Stuart.

STUART: Hello, Lillian, are you well?

LILLIAN: Yes, I'm fine, thank you.

STUART: Have you got a problem?

LILLIAN: My problem is my boyfriend, John.

STUART: Thought it might be.

LILLIAN: He's been very good to me. He's done lots of decorating for me. When we first started going out, we went a bit mad, went shopping on the plastic. Had a good time. And we got into debt and now we owe a lot of back rent, you see. And if we can't pay it we're going to be evicted. And we'll have nowhere to live…

Taxi arrives.

STUART: I'm struggling to hear you, Lillian.

LILLIAN: It's a bit noisy – that's another problem.

STUART: It is.

LILLIAN: Anyway. A friend of a friend of a friend –

STUART: That's a lot of friends you've got there, Lillian.

LILLIAN: Yeah –

STUART: Sorry. Go on.

LILLIAN: They've asked me to go to Amsterdam –

STUART: Amsterdam.

LILLIAN: To bring back a parcel in my little trolley –

STUART: What, sorry – a parcel.

LILLIAN: Yes, that's right.

STUART: Sounds dubious.

LILLIAN: It's cannabis –

STUART: Right.

LILLIAN: It's very good for you. Makes you eat.

STUART: Makes you eat confectionery from a twenty-four hour garage – and that's why it's illegal.

LILLIAN: Gives you the munchies. Makes you laugh.

STUART: Get to the point.

LILLIAN: The point is: it is illegal.

STUART: Yes it is.

LILLIAN: What about all these illegal refugees coming here? No one moans about them.

STUART: Well…

LILLIAN: So –

STUART: That depends where you stand. It is illegal.

LILLIAN: That's my problem – that's why I need your help.

STUART: We'll see what we can do, Lillian. Wait there, Lil.

We certainly will – let's pass it on to our contestants.

The video is paused.

What should Lillian do? Become a part of the international narcotics trade and pay off her debts, or live the rest of her life in poverty on the streets? What should she do?

He asks the audience and gets an answer.

Well, Lillian. The answer to your illegal problem, and of course cannabis is illegal and as such is against the law. The answer to your problem, Lillian is: (*He gives them the audience's answer.*)

LILLIAN: Ooh, thank you, Stuart!

STUART: Goodbye, Lillian!

There we are – you've made an old woman very happy!

Now, Ladies and Gentlemen, we're in for a very special treat tonight. We've got some very special guests all the way from Thespiana – I said Thespiana – all the way to see us tonight with a very special problem.

Ladies and gentlemen, from the Royal Shakespeare Company and the wider world of commercial theatre and bit-part television – Rory McGregor and Karen Paullada.

The next section contains the scene as played with the actors in the original production.

A musical sting and the two actors run on, waving.

Rory, Karen – pleased to meet you.

They sit on the sofa. STUART looks at RORY.

I recognise your face, don't I?

RORY: Spooks. I play Colin Wells.

STUART looks worried – he gets up.

STUART: No – get him out. Get him out!

He mimes being thrown about in a big explosion. Picks himself up in MI5 mode.

I want Special Powers!

Get me the Home Secretary!

He rushes to the sofa – with a mimed gun – and points it at RORY.

My priority now is to keep you on the sofa and ask you a few simple questions.

RORY doesn't say anything.

You've got the perfect face for espionage haven't you? Instantly forgettable.

He turns to KAREN.

And how about you, Karen?

KAREN: I played Beauty with the Royal Shakespeare Company.

STUART: You played an abstract noun – was that difficult?

KAREN: No. She's a character. In *Beauty and the Beast.*

STUART: In Shakespeare's *Beauty and the Beast*?

KAREN: It's not a Shakespeare play.

STUART: And you were doing it with the Royal Shakespeare Company?

Karen: Yes.

Stuart: But it's not a Shakespeare play. Not like: *Much Ado about Beauty.* Or: *Two Beauties of Verona.*

KAREN: No.

STUART: Not like: *Richard the Beauty.*

Not like: *Beauty for Beauty.*

KAREN: No, but –

STUART: Not like: *Henry the Beauty Part One.*

KAREN: Well –

STUART: Not like: *Henry the Beauty Part Two.*

No. Not a Shakespeare play – and not really as good.

So, Beauty, what's your problem?

KAREN: We're trying to do a play, but we haven't got enough actors.

STUART: You know what – I think we might be able to help you out. Is there anyone you think you can use out of that lot? Those four sitting there.

They each take a contestant by the hand: one takes a man from TREACLE's team, one takes the PLANT ACTOR – and they lead them off stage.

Well that's very exciting, isn't it? Whatever's going to happen next?

The actors playing HATTIE and ROB set up the contestant actors: the one playing ALEX in the tall cupboard, and the PLANT ACTOR playing CATHERINE off stage. As they set up, STUART talks to the audience.

Now this might look like an ordinary kitchen, but it is in fact a set. It's all been made especially for use in the theatre.

Much of it can be used just as you would use items at home. This chair, for example, is just like a normal chair – you can sit on it –

He sits on it. As he does so, SUGAR comes on and walks across with a plate of cream cakes.

It's quite comfortable.

(*STUART sees SUGAR.*) What's he got those for? Is that supposed to be a joke? Was that your idea? Don't ever parade cakes in front of me. Okay? I'm on a diet. Get the cakes off. Get the penguin off!

The penguin goes. The ACTOR PLAYING HATTIE signals that they're ready.

Ready? The actors are ready. So, as they say in the theatre:

He makes the clapperboard sign.

Action!

STUART scoots out of the way and exits.

SCENE THREE

ALEX – played by a member of the audience – and HATTIE are on. The scene from earlier repeats from this moment:

HATTIE opens the cupboard. ALEX is inside, on his mobile, still juggling all the sprouts.

ALEX: (*On the phone.*) Any minute. Just a minute. 'Bye.

He hangs up.

HATTIE: What are you doing?

ALEX comes out of the cupboard.

ALEX: That was Philippa. She's woken up. I've got to go home.

ROB comes back on, bumping into ALEX and sending him into HATTIE – he drops the sprouts. They spring apart.

ROB: Sorry!

HATTIE: Sorry.

ROB registers ALEX.

ROB: Alex –

They all pick up the sprouts and give them back to ALEX.

ALEX: Sorry.

ROB: Sorry about that.

ROB looks at ALEX holding the sprouts.

HATTIE: Just peel them, cut the bottoms and I'll do the rest. Twelve-thirty for one.

ROB: What?

HATTIE: Alex popped round for the sprouts.

ROB: Sprouts?

ALEX: Sprouts?

HATTIE: He's taking the sprouts. To prepare. I'm running very late.

ROB: What about the Sticky Toffee Pudding?

HATTIE: He says it's all under control.

ROB: Fancy you having Camp Coffee!

ALEX: Hattie –

HATTIE: Did you find the phone?

ROB: It had stopped ringing.

ALEX: I'd better –

He signals going.

ROB: Don't go on my account.

ALEX: No, no – of course not, no – never. No.

HATTIE: No!

> *She laughs, ALEX and ROB join in. A moment. The land line rings.*

ROB: 'Phone.

HATTIE: I'll get it.

> *We listen as HATTIE answers the phone.*

Hello?

Catherine.

ROB: Sunday lunch.

ALEX: Yeah.

HATTIE: Oh.

ROB: How long is it since we last had dinner together?

HATTIE: Oh dear.

ALEX: Is it a year?

ROB: Could be.

HATTIE: Don't worry. I'm sure he's somewhere.

ROB: Were you at ours last New Year?

ALEX: No. We were at home.

ROB: Course you were.

HATTIE: Of course. I'll have a look. And Rob will. And Alex is here. I'll tell him.

Okay?

You're all right.

'Bye.

> *HATTIE puts the phone down.*

It was Catherine. She can't find Rasputin.

ROB: Rasputin?

HATTIE: He hasn't come home for his breakfast.

> *ROB looks very worried.*

I said I'd tell you Alex.

ALEX: Good.

HATTIE: Have you seen him?

ROB: No.

He looks half-heartedly under the table, calling the cat.

Rasputin –

HATTIE: He's round here all the time.

ROB: Here puss, puss…

HATTIE: Sleeps on our bed.

ROB: Here puss, puss –

HATTIE: Rob doesn't like him.

ROB: It's not that I don't like him. Rasputin!

ROB sneezes five or more times in a row.

HATTIE: He hates cats.

ROB: I don't hate him.

He continues looking.

HATTIE: And above all he hates Rasputin.

ROB: I don't hate him at all.

ALEX: Do you like Buster?

HATTIE: He likes dogs.

ROB: Rasputin uses our garden as a big litter tray, that's all I said.

HATTIE: You said you wanted Rasputin dead –

ROB: (*Shouts.*) I don't want Rasputin dead!

I never said I want Rasputin dead!

ROB sneezes once.

I never said that!

ALEX: I've heard you –

To HATTIE.

I've heard him say he wants him dead!

HATTIE: He's heard you.

ROB: I didn't mean I wanted him dead. I just meant –

ALEX: What?

HATTIE: What?

ROB: I don't see why I should spend my life cleaning up after
someone else's filthy cat in my own home and be happy

about it. I should go and tell Catherine, nice as she is, that she's spoilt her cat so much she's turned it into a monster and, as much as I like her as a neighbour, Rasputin is completely out of control and should not be allowed to behave the way he does that in other people's homes and gardens – especially when I've put a lot of time and money into our garden and hers is a perfect cat litter tray.

ALEX: He's got a point.

The doorbell rings.

ROB: I'll go.

ROB exits.

HATTIE: Please don't, Alex. Please don't say it. Please don't say anything. Not now.

ROB enters with CATHERINE, played by the PLANT ACTOR.

Catherine.

ALEX: Catherine.

ROB: It's Catherine.

HATTIE: Have you found Rasputin?

CATHERINE: No.

HATTIE: Oh you poor thing, come and sit down.

She sits CATHERINE on the sofa.

CATHERINE: I can't find Rasputin anywhere.

HATTIE: When did you last see him?

CATHERINE: Last night.

ROB looks very uncomfortable. HATTIE moves a cushion to make CATHERINE more comfortable – revealing the dead cat behind it. ROB sees it, but nobody else does.

HATTIE: Maybe he's gone for a wander.

CATHERINE: I gave him a Marks's Risotto instead of the fish pie, and he hasn't even come back for his breakfast.

ROB: He'll be fine

CATHERINE: He always comes back for his breakfast.

ROB: He's absolutely fine.

HATTIE: He could be anywhere. He sleeps on our bed.

CATHERINE: Does he?

ALEX: We all have our little secrets.

ROB: He might be there now.

HATTIE: I don't think he is.

ROB: Have a look.

CATHERINE: Do you mind if we have a look?

HATTIE: Course not. Come on.

They all exit, leaving ROB. He jumps up and gets the cat off the sofa. Runs about with it – where to put it. Hears voices, off.

We'll go and look in the garden.

ALEX and HATTIE enter.

ALEX: Hattie –

HATTIE: Please, Alex, not now.

ALEX: This is very difficult for me.

HATTIE: I can see that, Alex.

They exit to the garden. ROB comes out from behind the sofa with the dead cat. He is about to make a bolt for the front door when CATHERINE enters, looking for the cat.

CATHERINE: Rasputin?

ROB shoves the cat in the washing machine.

Rob?

ROB: Catherine?

ALEX and HATTIE come in again.

HATTIE: He's not in the shed.

CATHERINE: I think something's happened to him.

ROB: Rasputin?

ALEX: Do you think there's been an accident?

CATHERINE: An accident?

ROB: No!

HATTIE: What sort of accident?

ROB: How does he know?

ALEX: I don't know –

ROB: He doesn't know –

HATTIE: He might have been run over.

CATHERINE: Rasputin – no!

CATHERINE runs off.

HATTIE: Catherine –

HATTIE runs after her.

ALEX: Hattie –

ALEX runs after her.

ROB: (*Quiet.*) Rasputin.

ROB goes to the washing machine and gets Rasputin out. One of the boxes with the actor in it starts to move. Subtly at first – hopefully the audience notice and there is a response: 'TREACLE' or 'HONEY'. Until this happens, ROB looks for somewhere to hide the cat. The audience response to the boxes breaks the scene, and STUART comes back on.

The actors exit as STUART sits on the box and tries to stop the person escaping. He gets the acting contestants – the PLANT ACTOR and the man – to sit on the box with him.

STUART: That's the one! He's in here! Let's get him off to Passport Control. Eh?

Well spotted [*Treacle/Honey's*] team! And well done to our two lovely actors.

What did we think of them? Should they have some points? How many?

How many points for [*name of male contestant*]. Five? Fifteen?

He increases the points until they stop encouraging him.

Lovely.

(*To male contestant.*) And how many cream horns can you eat at a sitting?

CONTESTANT: [*Number.*]

STUART: Disgusting.

And what about for Bola? Two? Twenty?

He increases the points until they stop encouraging him.

Give them a round of applause.

He lies across the box, trying to stop it opening.

And on top of those points – there's someone in the box!

That's one hundred points to [*Honey/Treacle's*] team.

Musical sting.

Is someone going to come and give me a hand?

Well done to you, [*Honey/Treacle's*] team.

Or shall I spend the rest of the show trying to control the UK's immigration problem with my arse?

The STAGE MANAGER comes on and takes the box off with the person struggling inside it, shouting and protesting violently. This frees the actor in the box to get out ready to be PETER TILSON. STUART helps the contestants back to their seats on the front row. HONEY enters.

What have you got for us, Honey?

She points at a model aeroplane she's carrying. Then she points underneath it, and shows us a little person climbing up the underside of it – someone is smuggling themselves into the wheel bay.

Is that what I think it is, Honey?

HONEY nods.

Is that a person? A person climbing… No!

HONEY nods, vociferously.

Climbing up onto the wheel arch? Unbelievable.

(*Shouts to the model person.*) Don't do it!

There he goes – there he is –

Laughs.

I don't know… Climbing up the wheel… And he's in. Here we go –

Sound of the 'plane taking off as HONEY animates it.

There he is.

Now what Honey wants to know is: how long does he last? How long does he last in the wheel base of the 777? You can confer, and write down for me: how long does he last in the wheel bay. Does he survive the flight?

Laughs.

Deary me. Timer, please!

Timer music starts. STUART comments on the journey as HONEY flies the plane.

The chicken or the beef? The chicken or the beef.

Range of perfumes and chocolates coming round on the duty free trolley.

When you go for a number two and flush it – what happens to the turd?

Answers on a postcard –

Time runs out.

For fifty points – and here tonight to tell us that all important answer, is Three Shires Security Firm Worker – Peter Tilson!

Music and on he comes.

Come on, Peter. Peter from Ealing.

STUART does the thumbs up/down thing and PETER tries to do it back.

You're a security guard, Peter?

PETER: Yes.

STUART: What do you guard?

PETER: I guard the store. The products in the store.

STUART: So you're the man making sure we get our baked beans for tea?

PETER: Yeah.

STUART: Making sure no-one nicks them. And those special things for cleaning saucepans?

PETER: Scourers.

STUART: Great job.

Peter – thanks for joining us tonight on Puzzles – Problems. And of course this particular journey was fraught with all sorts of Problems and Puzzles, wasn't it?

PETER: It was, Stuart.

STUART: So tell us, Peter, how had all this come about?

PETER tells us the story – with interceptions from STUART.

PETER: The guy was from Pakistan and he went to work in Dubai, but his employer took his passport and he couldn't get away, and he wasn't paid much money. He came from a really poor area in Pakistan – people are subsistence farmers – with barely enough to eat –

STUART: Barely enough to eat –

He turns to the audience.

That's just a dream for us, isn't it? Imagine ending every day having had barely enough to eat? We wouldn't have all these problems with obesity and ill health. Heart disease and people who can't run for a bus or even go under the surgeon's knife. We risk our lives every day with food. It should have a warning on it like matches: Don't Play With Food.

STUART looks back at PETER who doesn't respond. After a moment, PETER starts his story again.

PETER: His family's back in Pakistan and he's getting desperate, he wants them to get a good education and life. But it wasn't happening, so he escaped to another country next door called Bahrain – he was desperate really –

STUART: Where he found a plane.

PETER: A Boeing 777.

STUART: Big plane.

PETER: This rumour was going around that there's a secret hatch from the wheel bay into the cargo bay –

STUART: The wheel bay being the area beneath the plane that contains the wheels?

PETER: Yeah.

This guy must've thought he could get into the passenger cabin – but – I suppose it's only when he saw the wheels retracting up, and he managed not to get crushed by them, that he realised what he was getting into.

STUART: So he's inside the wheel bay? The plane takes off. It leaves the ground.

PETER: About ten minutes after take-off, he'd be freezing.

59

STUART: Bbrrrr!

PETER: Then a few minutes later, eighteen thousand feet
– there's no oxygen and you start to hallucinate. There's no
pressure –

STUART: There's no oxygen, there's no pressure –

PETER: The guy was just trying to get somewhere better.

He'd have been happy with my job.

He just wanted a better job to support his family.

STUART: I'd be happy with your job.

So he arrives in England – how does he end up in your car
park?

PETER: We're right under the flight path. All the planes go over
there.

And when the plane was coming down, the captain opened
the undercarriage and lowered the wheels –

STUART: And down he came. And there's a school?

PETER: There's a school right behind us.

STUART: And not one full of little penguins either. Could've
been really nasty.

PETER: It was really nasty.

STUART: So what are you thinking –

He laughs.

When you come into work and find this man lying in the car
park?

Because it was you found him.

PETER: I thought he was a drunk having a kip. And he's not the
only one –

STUART: You're joking!

PETER: We've had four.

STUART: Four.

So we're looking for an answer: how long, in those
conditions, was it before he died? We've got two teams and
they'll give us their best answers. And we'll see who gets the
fifty points. What've we got. What do you reckon?

Honey's Team –

HONEY's Team say their answer.

[*Honey's Team's answer*], say Honey's team. Treacle's team –

TREACLE's team say their answer.

Treacle's team reckon [*Treacle's Team's answer*]. Peter, can you give us the answer?

PETER: Ten minutes.

STUART: The economic migrant died just ten minutes into his journey.

And the fifty points go to: [*Treacle/Honey's*] Team.

Music.

And you've got a final bonus question for the winning team, haven't you, Peter?

PETER: I have.

STUART: How many points do [*Treacle/Honey's*] team get if they get this little puzzler right?

PETER: Fifty.

STUART: *Getting audience to join in.* Ooh! For another fifty points. [*Treacle/Honey's*] Team.

PETER gets some lumpy liquid in a clear plastic bag out of a supermarket bag.

Your question?

PETER: What's that.

STUART: What's that. For fifty points, your bonus question is:

PETER: What's this.

STUART: What is that. Fifty points at stake here – what have we got?

[*Treacle/Honey's*] team?

[TREACLE/HONEY'S] TEAM: We think it's [*answer*].

STUART: [*Answer.*] Peter?

PETER: It's his brains.

STUART: His brains?

PETER: We thought it was vomit, but it's his brains.

STUART: That's [*no points/fifty points*] to [*Treacle/Honey's*] team.

PETER: All he wanted was to get over here to make some money for his family.

STUART: And he got over here.

PETER: He was dead.

STUART: Well done. Thank you, Peter Tilson.

He encourages PETER towards the exit.

PLANT ACTOR: I think that's sick.

STUART: What?

PLANT ACTOR: It's sick.

STUART: No, it's his brains. We've just established that. He thought it was sick – but it's his brains.

STUART and the PLANT ACTOR continue an improvised argument along the lines of the script.

PLANT ACTOR: You've gone too far now. You've just gone over the mark.

STUART: Come on, it's nearly the interval. Go on – have a vodka and tonic.

PLANT ACTOR: There are some things you don't joke about. You shouldn't joke about things like this. You shouldn't be laughing about it.

STUART: Have an ice cream in a little tub with a spoon. I will. Who cares?

SUGAR enters and lunges towards STUART. The STAGE MANAGER tackles him, bringing him to the floor, and drags him off by his feet. STUART, too busy with his exchange with the PLANT ACTOR, who continues to rail at him, hardly notices.

PLANT ACTOR: You don't know what you're talking about.

STUART: Not a good game player!

PLANT ACTOR: I'm going to complain.

STUART: (*To the audience.*) Not a good sport. Sorry about that, ladies and gents.

The ACTOR PLAYING STUART comes out of character and casts around for someone to tell him what to do – genuinely worried. The PLANT ACTOR continues to rail at him.

Let's carry on. Keep going.

He does a funny dance for a moment.

Let's have the final scores, shall we?

Where are those animals – never about when you need them.

Where's Treacle? Or Honey? Honey!

He speaks into his microphone.

Where's Treacle? Treacle?

The PLANT ACTOR starts to leave, going to front of house. She aims a few last comments at STUART over her shoulder as she goes. As she goes the ACTOR PLAYING ROB peeps round the side of the set with the dead cat prop – not sure whether to continue or not – or whether his help is needed. He might find it wryly amusing. He goes off again. STUART has had enough – he exits. Once the PLANT ACTOR is out of the theatre, the ACTOR PLAYING ROB comes on in character. He resumes the moment where the play left off: ROB looking for somewhere to hide the cat.

HATTIE: (*Off.*) It's ten past twelve –

ROB puts the cat in the Le Creuset. HATTIE enters.

I've got to get the potatoes on.

She indicates the Le Creuset.

Is that the winter veg?

ROB: Yes.

She takes it from him. He tries to hide the chopped vegetables that are still on the table – or maybe they were put into the Le Creuset earlier by HATTIE, and now ROB has emptied them into a drawer.

HATTIE: Are you going to lay the table?

ROB doesn't want to leave her with the Le Creuset.

ROB: Not yet.

HATTIE: They'll be here any minute.

She puts the Le Creuset on the side.

No starters. Main course. Pudding. Plates and serving dishes ready to go in the oven. Serving spoons and glasses on the table.

ROB: Serving spoons.

HATTIE: And glasses. Drinks and nibbles in the sitting room.

What about salt and pepper?

ROB: I'll put it on the table.

He picks up the salt and pepper.

HATTIE: I mean this.

ROB: Me? No.

She takes the lid off the Le Creuset and – never taking her angry gaze from him – seasons the cat with the salt and pepper. He winces visibly as he sees what she's doing. She puts the lid back on and picks up the Le Creuset. ROB and HATTIE look at each other.

Hattie –

HATTIE: Drinks. Nibbles. Sitting room.

ROB: Drinks.

ROB exits to the sitting room to sort out the drinks. Before HATTIE can put the Le Creuset in the oven, there is the same cooing noise that we heard earlier from outside the back door.

HATTIE: No!

She listens make sure ROB has really gone.

ROB: (*Off.*) Hattie!

ALEX cooes again.

HATTIE: No –

The body of a MIGRANT falls into the kitchen from the roof. At no point does HATTIE acknowledge it. As it falls, a bright white light flashes out into the audience so that they can no longer see the stage. Then black. Interval. When the lights come up for the audience to exit, the actors have gone – but the body is still there. It's good to establish that it's a dummy.

ACT TWO

We return to the play exactly where we left it, with HATTIE holding the Le Creuset. The body that fell at the end of Act One is still on the floor, motionless. She doesn't see it. ROB enters.

ROB: What were you thinking of? Nibbles-wise?

HATTIE: Crisps.

ROB: Tortillas?

HATTIE: Kettle chips. And nuts. And I bought some of those mini-popadums. And mini-pretzels.

ROB: Mini-pretzels.

HATTIE: They're in the top cupboard.

I'll get them.

ROB indicates the Le Creuset.

ROB: Shall I hold that for you?

HATTIE: This?

ROB: Yes.

HATTIE gives him the Le Creuset – he's relieved, clutches it. HATTIE is amazed. She looks at him.

HATTIE: You haven't offered to do anything for me for ages.

ALEX coos again from outside the back door.

ROB: Haven't I?

HATTIE: Don't you know that?

ROB doesn't know what to say. ALEX coos again from outside the back door.

(*To the back door.*) Shut up!

The cooing stops – ROB is nonplussed. HATTIE stares at him.

What's happening to us, Rob?

ROB: The same things Hattie, over and over again.

HATTIE: We've got such a lovely house.

ROB: I know.

HATTIE: I thought we'd be happier.

ROB: It'll be okay, Hattie.

HATTIE: When, Rob?

The doorbell rings. ROB is still holding the Le Creuset.

ROB: I'll get it.

He starts to leave with the Le Creuset.

HATTIE: What about the winter veg?

She indicates the Le Creuset.

ROB: Winter veg?

HATTIE: Shall I put it in the oven?

ROB: Oven.

HATTIE: To cook.

ROB thinks he might confess about the cat.

ROB: Hattie?

HATTIE: Yes Rob?

They stand in silence for a bit. The doorbell rings again.

ROB: They're here.

HATTIE takes the Le Creuset from ROB. He watches her, pained, as she puts it in the oven. She shuts the oven door and smiles at him – he tries to smile back. The doorbell rings again. ROB exits to answer it. As the on-stage scene continues, we hear STUART and ROB in the hallway. There is cooing from the back door.

HATTIE: You can't come in.

ALEX comes in.

ALEX: Is Phil here?

HATTIE: No.

ALEX comes over to HATTIE.

ALEX: Let me hold you.

HATTIE: What about Rob?

ALEX: Don't talk about Rob.

HATTIE: What about Philippa?

ALEX: What about me?

HATTIE: I'm not married to you.

ALEX: What's marriage?

HATTIE: It's a legal document –

ALEX: What about you and me having someone to hold, when the world's not how we expected it to be?

He moves towards her – to hold her in his arms. She moves away from him, round the kitchen.

HATTIE: It's not how I expected.

ALEX: We're in pain. Events are causing us pain.

HATTIE: This isn't how it should be.

ALEX: We need a bit of comfort.

ROB: (*Approaching from off.*) Make yourself at home, Stu.

HATTIE dodges ALEX; ROB is returning.

ALEX: That's why we need each other.

HATTIE: Not now –

HATTIE bundles ALEX into the tall cupboard as ROB enters, to get a bottle of wine.

ROB: Stuart's here.

HATTIE: Good.

ROB: Alex and Phil haven't arrived yet.

HATTIE: Haven't they?

ROB: Do you think he's having trouble with the Sticky Toffee Pudding?

The MIGRANT who fell from the sky in Act One begins to move – gaining consciousness. Imperceptibly at first. So that the audience reaction is very disparate. There is a knock at the back door.

Who's that?

HATTIE looks – it can't be ALEX.

HATTIE: Catherine.

ROB moves out of the way of the back door – he doesn't want to see CATHERINE.

ROB: Catherine?

HATTIE moves out of the way too – she doesn't want CATHERINE at her party.

HATTIE: Ignore her.

ROB: Why?

HATTIE: She's not invited.

ROB: Isn't she?

We hear CATHERINE sobbing. The MIGRANT moves into a sitting position, head on knees. Obviously not well. When any of the characters notice him, the rule is that it's as if they're the only one who sees him – and he shouldn't be there. Like a fly. They look pissed off at him.

She's very upset.

HATTIE: We've hardly seen Stuart since he moved. This is the fourth time we've invited him round this year and it's the first time he's accepted. You know he doesn't like Catherine.

ROB: Doesn't he?

HATTIE: You know he doesn't.

ROB: Do I?

HATTIE: He thinks she's greedy and narcissistic.

ROB: Stuart does?

HATTIE: And he gets angry –

ROB: Does he?

HATTIE: And I get indigestion.

ROB: Do you?

HATTIE: Why do you think we've got Rennie's in the bathroom cabinet?

The MIGRANT moves to sit against a kitchen cabinet.

ROB: I don't know.

HATTIE: You don't know the first thing about me.

The doorbell rings. ROB exits to answer it. HATTIE kicks the MIGRANT.

Get out of the way.

The MIGRANT shifts over. It's PHIL at the door. As the scene on-stage continues, we hear her enter – off – and be taken into the sitting room. She has already been drinking. HATTIE opens ALEX's cupboard.

HATTIE: Your wife's here.

ALEX: Where?

HATTIE: In the sitting room. You have to go out the back door, round the front and come in properly.

ALEX: I know. I will.

HATTIE: Now.

ALEX: Come here.

HATTIE: No!

ALEX: Let me hold you –

He grabs her as ROB enters, calling to PHIL who is in the sitting room – off.

ROB: (*Off.*) We've got another white in the fridge.

HATTIE tries to get ALEX off and get him in the cupboard – he interprets this as a passionate advance and makes the most of it.

ALEX: Yes –

HATTIE: Alex –

ALEX: Hattie –

HATTIE: No –

She bundles him in to the cupboard – he takes her with him and the door shuts behind them as ROB comes in. He is surprised to find the kitchen empty.

ROB: Hattie?

He takes the opportunity to take the Le Creuset out of the oven and get the cat out. In his desperation to get it out, he does it with his bare hands. It's very hot. He tries to think where to put it – STUART enters – it's the first time we've seen him in this act – we recognise him from the game show.

STUART: What do you think?

ROB: Sorry?

STUART turns to the side to show his profile.

STUART: Stay trim. Get more quim. Any more white?

ROB: Yes, it's in the –

He doesn't have any hands free to get it.

STUART: You've put on haven't you, Rod?

The Le Creuset is becoming painful to hold, but ROB seems welded to it – unable to think what to do.

ROB: Rob.

STUART: Were you always that size?

ROB is wincing.

If you're going to have a car like mine, you've got to look good.

He indicates out of the window at his car. ROB is in pain.

You know the biggest turnoff? When a Merc SL pulls up and some fat dick gets out. If you can't look good getting out of your own car – get the fucking bus.

The MIGRANT, who we have almost forgotten about, vomits. The characters look at him occasionally, disgusted.

ROB: There's someone in your car, Stu. In the driver's seat.

STUART looks. ROB takes the opportunity to douse the Le Creuset in the sink. There is steam.

STUART: That's my driver for the day. I'm not driving at the moment.

STUART turns back and sees ROB and the steam. ROB pretends to be washing salad in the sink.

ROB: I'm just washing the cat –

STUART: The cat?

ROB: The salad!

ROB puts the cat into a tea-towel which he spins around, as though preparing salad. He laughs. STUART laughs. The MIGRANT gets up and crosses the room.

STUART: Washing the cat!

ROB: The cat! We haven't even got a cat.

STUART: But you have got salad?

ROB: Salad we have got.

ROB sees the MIGRANT coming and whacks him deliberately with the spinning salad. He falls/staggers. The cat's face is peeping out from the tea towel.

STUART: And presumably a few other comestibles – seeing as you've invited us for lunch.

ROB tries to divert attention from the cat.

ROB: He's getting out. Your driver.

STUART: So he is.

ROB tries to wrap the cat up again.

ROB: He's walking up and down.

STUART: Right again.

He grabs a colander to put over it.

ROB: He's waving.

STUART waves.

STUART: (*In a silly voice.*) Hello!

ROB: He's coming over.

STUART: (*In a silly voice.*) What do you want, Mister Sunday Driver?

ROB: He's coming to the door.

The doorbell sounds. ROB looks at STUART. STUART looks away. ROB exits to the door with the cat in the tea towel and the colander.

STUART: Note to self: Starting to feel very fucking hungry.

Note to self: Dinner will be served in –

He looks at his watch, agitated.

Twenty-four minutes.

The MIGRANT staggers about, bumping into things – narrowly avoiding the characters at times.

Note to self: You've eaten the mini-popadums and mini-pretzels. Try to hold on.

Note to self: fuck off.

STUART turns to the MIGRANT.

Will you get out of my fucking field of vision?

The MIGRANT looks at STUART, he does not move. STUART nuts the MIGRANT. The MIGRANT falls to the floor. ROB enters.

ROB: He wants to know how long you'll be?

STUART: I don't know.

ROB: He said he thought you were only going for a spin.

STUART: (*Shouts down the hallway, in silly voice.*) I don't know!
I haven't had me dinner yet!

ROB: I've asked him in.

STUART: (*Pissed off.*) That's your call.

(*Aside.*) Note to self: Do not ever fucking come here again.

ROB: That's not a problem, is it?

STUART: Not for me, Bob.

ROB: Rob.

STUART: (*Sarcastic.*) Now, can anyone remember what I came in
here for?

ROB: Urm –

STUART: Was it a bottle of white wine?

ROB: Of course.

*ROB tries to open the fridge while holding the cat arrangement.
The MIGRANT gets up.*

There's one in here. Help yourself.

*STUART takes the bottle of wine out. The MIGRANT staggers in.
ROB watches him and shuts the door.*

STUART: Phil polished off the last one. She thinks Alex is having
an affair.

ROB: Alex?

STUART: Well – stranger things happen.

The doorbell goes.

ROB: I'd better just –

STUART: Be my guest –

*They move to stand looking off to the front door as HATTIE tries
to get out of the cupboard – but ALEX is pulling her back. HATTIE
and ALEX speak over STUART and ROB, who speak over PHIL
and CATHERINE. Some bumping and banging as PHIL tries to
answer the door.*

/ Phil's got it – no she hasn't – that's the coat hooks, Phil.
Keep going – other side – now she's got it.

ROB: Thanks, Phil.

PHIL answers the front door and we hear CATHERINE – off – as HATTIE speaks.

CATHERINE: / Phil – where's Hattie? I can't find Rasputin. I've looked everywhere. He never does this – I just want to find Rasputin.

HATTIE: Get off me –

She hits ALEX, but he hangs on.

Get off –

ALEX manages to get HATTIE back into the cupboard and the door shut as STUART exits and ROB turns back into the room with the cat in the tea towel. Neither STUART nor ROB are pleased at CATHERINE's arrival.

ROB: Catherine –

ROB comes back into the room with the cat in the tea towel, panicking.

STUART: (*Off.*) Oh dear.

ROB puts the cat into the fruit basket where it sits among the fruit – with just its head peeping out between oranges and apples. We hear CATHERINE crying some more. ROB dives into a cupboard. As he does so, SUGAR the penguin crowbars his way in through the window. We don't know it's him at first – until he squeezes himself through the window. He is clutching a rifle wrapped in a cloth – we can't really make out what it is – he wears a beard as a disguise. He looks around – orientating himself. The fridge opens and the MIGRANT comes out. SUGAR turns on him with the rifle and backs him back into the fridge, closing the door after him. STUART is approaching.

(*Off.*) I'll ask Mein Host.

SUGAR hops into an uninhabited cupboard as STUART enters. The kitchen's empty.

Oh.

STUART is surprised. He sees the Le Creuset on the side. He approaches it, having an inner battle with himself.

Open the lid.

No.

You know you want to.

No I don't.

You know you're hungry.

I'm not hungry.

You've eaten all the Kettle chips.

I did not.

You hid the salted cashews from Phil and Catherine so you could eat them when they weren't looking.

I'm never hungry.

And the pistachios. And that floral Bombay Mix.

I feel no hunger.

And you made Peter stop on the way at that garage so you could get a Ginster's pasty.

I hate you.

I hate you too, fattie. Lift the lid.

I will not lift the lid.

Showing huge self-control, STUART wrenches himself away from the Le Creuset and exits. HONEY and TREACLE enter through the audience. They are not their normal happy-go-lucky selves. They are very worried. They are looking for SUGAR. This can overlap with STUART's previous entrance as long as he doesn't notice them. They come down onto the stage to continue their search. They mime their reactions to each other: big head shakes, shrugs, hands over faces in worry...they could even mime shouting to him. The essence of their mimed conversation is:

- WHERE IS HE?

- I DON'T KNOW.

- HE CAME IN HERE.

- SO WHERE IS HE NOW?

- I CAN'T SEE HIM ANYWHERE.

- WHAT ARE WE GOING TO DO?

- HE'S LOOKING FOR STUART.

- I KNOW.

- SUGAR HATES STUART.

- I KNOW.

- HE'S GOT A GUN.

- I KNOW.

- WHAT SHALL WE DO?

- WE HAVE TO WARN STUART.

- GOOD IDEA.

As the animals are getting desperate, STUART enters. He is heading for the Le Creuset when he sees them. He is not happy to see them and they are desperate to communicate with him. Think Lassie with a crap owner.

What do you think you're doing here?

They try to communicate why they've come.

Are you invited?

They try to communicate why they've come.

Have you been invited?

They look at each other and shake their heads.

No. These people invited me – not you. No-one's interested in you.

One of them tries to warn him.

You come on the show. Fine. But that's as far as it goes.

As he continues, they try to mime a disaster involving SUGAR, but STUART doesn't get it.

You're seriously over-estimating how important you are to me.

Problems – Puzzles, Puzzles – Problems is the Stuart White show. It's not the bear, penguin and what are you – rabbit show. It's not your show. It's not our show – it's my show.

STUART's starting to get to them now – they are not very thick-skinned.

I could have you replaced like that.

He clicks his fingers.

I could have you replaced with a – a llama, a koala and…a donkey – and no one would notice. Go away. Go on. Find some furry friends of your own. No one here wants to see you. We don't want you here. Get out – go on. Stupid animals.

Their heads hang – should get some audience response – STUART can respond by grabbing TREACLE by the ears.

(*To the audience.*) You don't want me to send them home from a private party, but if I skinned him and fried him with some onions you'd gobble him up!

He can tell the audience to shut up if he wants.

Fuck off. That's the way – fuck off.

He shoos the animals – pushing them out of the back door. After a few final attempts to communicate, they exit. As they do, we hear CATHERINE crying, off.

Please, not Catherine.

CATHERINE enters, sobbing. It's the first time we've seen the actor since presuming they were an audience member. STUART doesn't react to this. As she enters, he winces. He remains with his back to the door.

CATHERINE: When Ben left. I thought I'd always be alone.

STUART stands, looking grim – still doesn't turn around. He thinks if he stays still, she might shut up or go away.

Then about a week later, I was in the kitchen and I'd just done myself a Marks's Cod and Smoked Haddock Pie when Rasputin walked through the back door.

He starts to pull faces, mimicking and taking the piss out of her.

He came straight over. And he sniffed. And he sat down. And without even looking at me, he started to eat from my plate.

She trails off and cries again. He looks at his watch.

He chose me.

He starts to open the back door and escape silently.

Have you ever felt like that, Stuart?

STUART freezes.

STUART: Absolutely.

CATHERINE spots something on the floor. She bends down and picks it up.

CATHERINE: This is his bell.

STUART: Is it?

CATHERINE: So I knew when he was coming.

STUART: Good idea.

CATHERINE looks at the bell. She is even more upset. She cries. We know that all the others are listening in the cupboards. PETER TILSON enters. He has the same wine bottle we saw STUART exit with, now empty, and is having trouble with PHIL, who's upset and increasingly drunk. CATHERINE still cries.

PETER: Is there anyone called Alex in here?

CATHERINE cries.

STUART: No, mate.

PETER: Or Hattie.

CATHERINE cries.

CATHERINE / STUART: No.

STUART: Just us.

PETER: What about Rob?

STUART: For Christ's sake, what are you doing, James –

PETER: Peter.

STUART: Taking the register?

CATHERINE cries and cries.

PETER: There's someone in the sitting room called Phil –

STUART: Phil, yes.

PETER: She asked me to come and see if any of the people I mentioned are in here.

STUART: No they're not, David.

PETER: Peter. She seems very upset. And she'd like another glass of white wine.

STUART: Not a problem.

He looks in the fridge and then cupboards for some wine. Despite opening most of the cupboards, he doesn't see the people. When he opens the fridge, the MIGRANT tries to get out. STUART shuts the door. SUGAR is revealed taking a rifle from the cloth he brought on. STUART shuts the door, he doesn't see either of them. STUART finds a bottle of red wine. As he passes PETER, he whispers to him.

(Aside to PETER.) Boyfriend's left her. Sounds quite kinky.

He gives PETER a wink and exits with the bottle to the sitting room.

PETER: Sorry to hear.

CATHERINE shakes her head.

You don't think he's coming back?

CATHERINE: Everyone laughs at me because I feed him Marks and Spencers' meals, but he wouldn't eat anything else. And I didn't have any left last night. He just sniffed his plate and walked out and he often goes out after his dinner and sometimes he is out all night, but he's always back for his breakfast.

PETER: You've lost your cat.

CATHERINE: I thought he was cross with me about his dinner, but now I think something's happened to him.

Silence. A cupboard opens a chink – HATTIE and ALEX peep out.

I found the bell from his collar.

It closes again as they realise there are still people in the kitchen. CATHERINE shows him the bell.

People think it doesn't matter.

It's just a cat. You can get another one.

PETER: No.

CATHERINE: Nobody cares.

She's very upset. She stops. Silence. A cupboard opens a chink – ROB peeps out.

They make the right noises. But it doesn't matter to them.

It closes again.

PETER: No.

CATHERINE: He had a life. His own life. And now he's gone. And if a life has gone, that should matter.

PETER: It doesn't seem to, does it?

Silence. Two cupboards open a chink – ROB and HATTIE peep out – they don't see each other.

CATHERINE: Like he's nothing.

They close again. CATHERINE puts her hands over her face. She is silent. PETER pulls his chair over and puts a hand on her shoulder. Silence. HATTIE, ROB and SUGAR's cupboards all open together.

PETER: I know.

The cupboards all close.

CATHERINE: What sort of a world is this where a life counts for so little?

CATHERINE drops the bell. They both bend down to look for it. As they do so, all the others open their cupboard doors and step out of the cupboards in unison and shut their doors silently and immediately pretend to be busy. Except SUGAR, who comes out with his rifle, looks around, can't see STUART and goes back into his cupboard. The MIGRANT is still stuck in the fridge. PETER and CATHERINE come up to find the room full. People are surprised to see each other, with HATTIE, ROB and ALEX trying to act casual. ALEX goes to the sink. ROB looks at the fruit bowl.

ROB: Alex – you made it.

ALEX: Yeah!

ROB picks up the fruit bowl.

HATTIE: Has anyone seen the kettle?

PETER: No.

ROB: Can I get anyone a drink?

HATTIE: Where's Stuart?

PETER: He's in the sitting room with Phil.

ALEX: Phil.

HATTIE: Why doesn't everyone go through?

ROB: Good idea –

He picks up the fruit bowl and starts to usher everyone except HATTIE through to the sitting room.

HATTIE: What are you doing with the fruit?

ALEX and CATHERINE exit.

ROB: I was going to take it through to the sitting room. They're getting hungry.

HATTIE: They've got crisps.

ROB: They've eaten the crisps – and the nuts, and the pretzels. They've even eaten the pot pouri. Let's take them some fruit before they start on the sofa.

PETER is exiting.

HATTIE: Peter, would you mind taking the fruit through to the sitting room?

PETER: Course.

PETER takes the fruit from ROB.

HATTIE: Tell people to help themselves.

PETER exits to the sitting room with the fruit.

Can't we get rid of Catherine?

ROB: It was me.

HATTIE: That bloody woman and her filthy cat.

ROB: I killed Rasputin.

HATTIE: You.

ROB: I put the Le Creuset on top of him.

HATTIE: You monster.

ROB: He was in the sheets with the bird on.

HATTIE: You didn't have to kill him.

ROB: It was an accident. If he hadn't killed the bird and left it on our bed, the sheets wouldn't have been on the kitchen table he wouldn't have got in the sheets and I wouldn't have squashed him with the Le Creuset.

HATTIE: So it's the cat's fault it got killed?

ROB: Those are my sheets. That is my bed. Where I sleep. My Le Creuset. My kitchen.

Suddenly I'm committing murder by going about my normal daily business.

HATTIE: Where is he now?

ROB: He's in the fruit bowl.

HATTIE: The fruit bowl?

We hear CATHERINE scream, off, as they realise the full horror. Then the sound of concerned voices.

CATHERINE: No!

ROB and HATTIE rush to the back door, they open it and rush out as ALEX comes in from the sitting room. He looks round the room. It's empty.

ALEX: Hattie? Hattie!

He starts to look into cupboards.

Phil knows. She knows about us. I think you should tell Rob.

He opens the cupboard with SUGAR in it. He shouldn't be there.

THE ACTOR PLAYING ALEX: You're not meant to be in there. Who is that?

He tries to work out who's in the costume.

Who's in there? You shouldn't be in here.

SUGAR slowly points the rifle at him. The ACTOR PLAYING ALEX raises his hands slightly. SUGAR shuts his cupboard door. The ACTOR PLAYING ALEX exits to the sitting room. ROB and HATTIE enter again, from the back door.

HATTIE: Perhaps she's gone home.

ROB: What am I going to do?

HATTIE sees the joint of beef still on the side.

HATTIE: What's that?

ROB: It's a joint of beef.

HATTIE: Is it?

ROB: What's it doing there?

HATTIE: I've forgotten to cook it.

She looks at ROB.

ROB: You've forgotten to cook the beef?

HATTIE: We've got five people –

ROB: Seven. If you count Catherine. And Peter.

HATTIE: Seven people ready for Sunday dinner and we haven't got any roast.

ROB: What have we got? Sticky toffee pudding?

HATTIE: No.

ROB: Sprouts?

HATTIE: No. Winter veg?

ROB: No.

ROB: Salt and pepper –

He gets them and puts them on the table.

We've got salt and pepper. We've got a bag of salad.

He gets it out of the fridge. STUART enters. He is surprised to see them.

STUART: Have you got another bottle of white?

ROB: I think that was the last one.

STUART: Red?

HATTIE: There's one in the cupboard –

STUART: We've had that one.

ROB: I'll have a look under the stairs.

He goes. STUART stays.

STUART: Anything I can help you with?

HATTIE: No. I'm fine. Thank you.

STUART goes. She is left alone in the kitchen.

All I've done is try to make a nice lunch for my friends and my family. For other people.

What have I done to deserve this?

She shouts to the sky.

Why is this happening to me?!

The shout turns into the music for The Missing Link. It builds and NEIL, played by the ACTOR PLAYING ROB, enters from front of house and jogs into the audience, carrying a microphone.

We still see HATTIE, at her wits' end, as NEIL addresses us. She is alternately looking in cupboards, pulling her hair out, trying to overcome the problem and giving in to it. Sometimes frantic. Sometimes completely still. Oblivious to The Missing Link. She is tortured.

NEIL: Have you got a problem? Is there something in your life that's not going according to plan? Are things falling apart around you?

TREACLE and HONEY start to look through the audience for someone – they have video cameras on their heads, which show the audience on the video screen.

If you feel like you've got the weight of the world on your shoulders then I'm looking for you.

TREACLE takes his camera down onto the stage and we start to see HATTIE on the video screen. She is beating up the beef.

And I'm going to find you. And together we're going to play: The Missing Link.

A claxon sounds.

Treacle's found one. Treacle, who have you got for us?

HATTIE is in a state. TREACLE points at her punching the beef.

Look at that! Pick on someone your own size!

Can you hear me?

HATTIE can, but she looks at the camera – she speaks to the camera.

HATTIE: What?

NEIL: What's going on?

HATTIE: I've forgotten to cook the beef.

NEIL: Your beef is with the beef?

HATTIE: I haven't cooked it.

I've got people for lunch.

He comes down onto the stage. Still she talks to the camera. Finally he puts his arms round her and she registers him and starts to talk to him.

NEIL: And nothing to give them.

Do you think you've been kidding yourself a bit?

HATTIE nods.

Kidding yourself you can make a lovely Sunday lunch?

HATTIE: Yes.

NEIL: I'm Neil Richardson. What's your name?

HATTIE: Hattie Mullen.

NEIL: What sorts of things are you starting to realise now, Hattie?

HATTIE: That I can't.

NEIL: And how does it feel being honest about those things?

She starts to cry – NEIL is very sympathetic.

You're all tearful.

Hattie, you've taken the first step – you've admitted you've got a problem with your Sunday lunch.

Does that mean you'd like things to be different?

HATTIE: Yes.

NEIL: If you could change one thing, right now, with our help, what would it be?

HATTIE: I'd have a nice joint of meat on that table, ready for my guests.

NEIL: You want lunch?

HATTIE: Yes.

NEIL: More than anything else in the world at this moment: lunch.

HATTIE: Lunch, yes.

She nods and TREACLE takes her up into the audience.

NEIL: Ladies and gentlemen – our first contestant tonight – Hattie!

Let's see who you're playing tonight. Honey – where are you?

HONEY waves and listens.

Honey, the Missing Link is lunch. To play the game we need to find someone in the world who is linked to Hattie's lunch.

You ready, Honey?

HONEY nods.

Okay – you've got twenty seconds to find Hattie's Missing Lunch Link. Starting:

On the video screen we see the number 20.

now! As the counter counts down, Honey is going to find someone – could be anyone – who has a link with Hattie and also with her lunch.

HONEY runs off through the audience as the counter begins to count down from 20 to 1 and lights flash round the stage. Music plays.

Eight seconds left. Seven – six – five – four – three – two – one –

A claxon sounds.

She's done it!

The image on the video screen 'shatters' and we see a box at a deportation centre. HONEY is there.

Honey! Have you found the missing link?

She nods vehemently.

Ladies and gentleman – Hattie – she's found your Missing Link.

A musical sting. TREACLE brings NEIL a sealed envelope. The details of this new contestant are written on the outside of it.

Who have you got for us, Honey?

She points at the box as NEIL reads.

Our second contestant tonight is Bashkim from Albania.

HONEY opens the box and the migrant gets out. He speaks Albanian. We can't understand what he's saying.

NEIL: Hello Bashkim!

BASHKIM: (*In Albanian.*) Hello.

NEIL: What was that?

BASHKIM: (*In Albanian.*) I would very much like to stay here –

NEIL: I'm sorry –

TREACLE brings the translating device over to NEIL.

What's this, Treacle?

TREACLE mimes that it's a translating device. As he explains,
HONEY puts one onto BASHKIM on the video. She also sets up a
button for him to press in the game.

It's a device for simultaneously translating from any language
into English?

Isn't that fantastic?

NEIL addresses a member of the audience.

How are you with languages? Rubbish? That's perfect.
Because you don't need to know anything – this device will
give you an automatic translation of everything our Albanian
friend says. All you have to do is say, nice and loud, into
your microphone, exactly what you hear as soon as you hear
it. Treacle will help –

TREACLE sets the translating device up on the audience member.
It translates BASHKIM's voice into English. So the voice which the
audience member hears is BASHKIM's. It translates simultaneously
with BASHKIM speaking.

Bashkim. Hattie wants lunch for her family and friends.
Sunday lunch. Not a big ask. Not a fast car or a flash holiday.
So it's lunch that's on offer here, Bashkim – we're playing for
lunch. Do you want to play?

BASHKIM: (*In Albanian.*) Yes please.

TRANSLATION: Yes please.

NEIL: And who are you playing for lunch for, Bashkim?

BASHKIM: (*In Albanian.*) My / family.

TRANSLATION: My family.

NEIL: And why do you want lunch for your family? Have you
bungled the beef as well?

BASHKIM: (*In Albanian.*) My family / don't have enough.

TRANSLATION: My family don't have enough.

NEIL is shocked.

NEIL: Your own family.

How does it feel being honest about that now?

BASHKIM: (*In Albanian.*) It's / the truth.

TRANSLATION: It's the truth.

NEIL: I don't doubt it. So you want lunch for you and your family.

BASHKIM: (*In Albanian.*) Not for me. / Just my family. I left my family in Albania to earn some money so they can have better lives.

TRANSLATION: Not for me. Just my family. I left my family in Albania to earn some money so they can have better lives.

NEIL: Do you two know each other?

HATTIE: No.

BASHKIM shakes his head.

NEIL: Never met before. And yet, you do have something in common. Something that connects you both. And whichever one of you guesses the Missing Link that connects the two of you, wins the lunch. Okay? During our conversation, if you think you know what it is – press your button.

They nod. NEIL sets up a button for HATTIE.

Hattie, tell me about your morning.

HATTIE: It's been awful. Rob's killed Rasputin.

NEIL: That's the neighbour's cat.

HATTIE: Yes.

ALEX comes into the kitchen.

NEIL: (*Mock-quiet.*) Is this the neighbour?

HATTIE: No, that's another neighbour. Alex.

NEIL: The one you're having an affair with!

HATTIE: Oh!

NEIL: Don't worry – he can't hear you –

He shouts.

Alex – your secret's safe with us –

HATTIE: No!

NEIL: Can't hear a thing.

And how long have you been seeing Alex for?

HATTIE: Seven months.

NEIL: Don't worry, we won't tell a soul.

ALEX goes.

And this is a special lunch, isn't it, for a special guest.

HATTIE: Stuart White.

NEIL: Stuart White.

BASHKIM sounds his claxon.

Bashkim – do you know the missing link?

BASHKIM: Is it Stuart White / from Problems – Puzzles, Puzzles – Problems. Is he the link?

TRANSLATION: Is it Stuart White from Problems – Puzzles, Puzzles – Problems. Is he the link?

A 'negative' sound is heard, signifying that BASHKIM hasn't got the right answer.

NEIL: Good try – but no, Stuart White is not the missing link. How do you know Stuart White, Hattie?

HATTIE: He used to live next door but one to us. And then he moved.

NEIL: And you don't see him so much.

HATTIE: Yes, that's right.

NEIL: Bashkim – you're from Albania. How's your day been?

BASHKIM: (*In Albanian.*) I don't want / to be deported.

TRANSLATION: I don't want to be deported.

NEIL: You've been taken to a deportation centre. Tell us – why are you being deported, Bashkim?

BASHKIM: (*In Albanian.*) Because / I'm an illegal immigrant here.

TRANSLATION: Because I'm an illegal immigrant here.

HATTIE sounds her claxon.

NEIL: Hattie – you think you know what the link is?

HATTIE: I don't know – does Bashkim work at the Sainsbury's I go to?

The 'negative' sound is heard again, signifying that HATTIE hasn't got the right answer.

NEIL: No he doesn't.

CATHERINE comes into the kitchen, followed by PETER. She's holding the cat. NEIL, HATTIE, BASHKIM and the animals watch.

PETER: Where are you going?

CATHERINE: I'm leaving.

PETER: Don't.

CATHERINE holds Rasputin's body to her.

NEIL: Are these friends of yours?

HATTIE: They're not invited.

CATHERINE: They don't want me here.

HATTIE: That's the cat.

PETER: We're only here because they've messed things up for us.

NEIL: What – the cat Rob killed?

HATTIE: Yes.

PETER: Because Stuart conned me into driving his car here and they've killed your cat. We're not leaving now. That's exactly what they're hoping we'll do. You think we should let them off the hook?

CATHERINE: No.

PETER: We're going to stay and we're going to have lunch.

NEIL: They want lunch.

PETER: Come on.

NEIL: They're going.

CATHERINE and PETER go back through to the sitting room.

Bashkim, you're an illegal immigrant. You've taken a brave step telling us that. It is against the law – and we are all obliged to live by the law. The law is there to help us. To protect us. We can't do things just because we want to. What made you come over here, Bashkim, illegally – what made you break the law.

BASHKIM: (*In Albanian.*) My mother / has a farm in the North of Albania. We grow maize.

TRANSLATION: My mother has a farm in the North of Albania. We grow maize.

NEIL: That's a sort of corn, isn't it?

BASHKIM: (*In Albanian.*) It is. But / we can't grow enough, we can't sell enough. We need some money – so I came here.

TRANSLATION: It is. But we can't grow enough, we can't sell enough. We need some money – so I came here.

NEIL: And what happens to your maize?

BASHKIM: (*In Albanian.*) We eat some / and feed some to our animals – and we sell some at the market, when we can get there.

TRANSLATION: We eat some and feed some to our animals – and we sell some at the market, when we can get there.

HATTIE presses her button and the claxon sounds.

HATTIE: Is it the maize? Is the maize that Bashkim grows the missing link?

A celebratory sound and the lights dance.

NEIL: The Missing Link is the maize!

HATTIE is delighted. TREACLE shakes the audience member's hand, takes the microphone and translating device and goes.

Can you tell us why?

HATTIE: No.

NEIL takes the envelope from his pocket and opens it. He reads.

NEIL: The surplus maize that's grown on Bashkim's family farm is sold at the market, then exported to Croatia, where it's taken to a factory – along with a lot of other maize – and made into animal fodder, which is put onto the open market and regularly purchased by a cattle farmer in Fife. Hattie, what was your roast?

HATTIE: The beef!

NEIL: Beef raised on the very maize that Bashkim's family grew. So Bashkim, you've been providing Hattie's lunch. What a lovely Missing Link. You got it right, you've won. You've won a lovely lunch for your friends and family. How does that feel?

HATTIE: Brilliant!

NEIL: Bashkim. It was the maize.

BASHKIM shakes his head.

The maize your family have been growing.

BASHKIM looks devastated.

You had a go, Bashkim, you took a risk. It was a brave thing to do. But it didn't pay off this time.

On the screen, we see BASHKIM being taken away by two deportation officers.

Hattie?

HATTIE is giggly.

You've got the giggles. You did it.

HATTIE: I didn't think I would.

NEIL: Well done. And you know what this means?

HATTIE: The meat –

NEIL: Your guests are getting hungry and they've decided to come through to the kitchen. Let's see what happens next – you wait with me.

HONEY and BASHKIM disappear from the screen. HATTIE stays in the audience with NEIL.

HATTIE: No – I can't watch! Oh dear.

NEIL: Because your guests are all expecting a lovely Sunday lunch. They've whetted their appetites with a few glasses of Chardonnay – and then a few glasses of Rioja, and then I think they started on the Schnapps.

And now they're ready to eat –

Her guests come on: STUART, PETER, ALEX, CATHERINE.

HATTIE: Oh no.

NEIL: Here they come. Here's Alex. Blow him a kiss – only joking. Here's Stuart.

The guests chat – but we can't really hear what they're saying.

I think your presence is required, Hattie – ladies and gentlemen, give it up for Hattie Mullen.

NEIL leads the applause as HATTIE goes back into her own life.

HATTIE: What about the joint?

NEIL: Hattie – you're going to have to make this journey on your own.

Down you go.

She walks down like a star. Gets plates out of the oven and puts them onto the table. People are sitting down and chatting. HATTIE is beside herself with worry. CATHERINE is very upset, but comforted by PETER.

HATTIE: Shall I open the salad? There's salt and pepper on the table.

STUART: Where do you want me?

HATTIE: Anywhere you like, Stuart.

STUART: Ooh – er.

ALEX: Phil's having a lie down.

HATTIE: Shall I open the salad?

The body of BASHKIM falls onto the dinner table. Nobody reacts.

STUART: Shall I be Mother?

HATTIE: Thank you, Stuart.

They pull back the jacket and carve it – it's BASHKIM. We can see by his clothes. People pass plates. The Sunday lunch begins – as if everything is perfectly normal. Music starts – as we will find out, it's the introduction to a song. HATTIE's worry disappears. ROB enters and joins the others at the table.

Rasputin starts to come alive – CATHERINE can hardly hold him – he launches himself through the air, claws outstretched. He lands on ROB's face and starts to claw it off, sending ROB crashing around the stage, then out into the audience trying to rip the cat off his face. This causes chaos at the table as CATHERINE chases ROB and the cat. HATTIE chases them and ALEX chases HATTIE. They run round and round – HATTIE trying to get ALEX off her, CATHERINE trying to get the cat – and attack ROB too when it looks like he might hurt the cat. ROB's face getting more and more bloody. As this chase continues, we lose HATTIE, who changes into TREACLE. ALEX will ultimately take over as SUGAR. PETER is drawing STUART's attention to everything that's going on around him, but STUART is much more interested in eating everything he can. He barely bothers to look up.

TREACLE enters and starts to sing. As in Act One, the words appear on the video screen, with a bouncy ball to orientate the audience.

TREACLE: (*Sings.*) Nothing else quite packs a punch
Like a free market global lunch.
Watch the whole of life unfurl –
Pull up a chair and eat the world.

Throughout the song, we see images on the screen of the audience, of parts of the chases that are going on off-stage, of people in other countries crowding round. Things that are disturbing. Useless products. Huge amounts of food.

You're everso everso close this time
To feeling really almost fine.
You're really nearly really happy
Nearly really really happy.
Really nearly happy.

Juicy peaches in December
It's one big consumption bender –
If you can satiate your greed,
Your satisfaction's guaranteed.

You're everso everso close this time
To feeling really almost fine.
You're really nearly really happy
Nearly really really happy.
Really nearly happy.

Looking for ROB, CATHERINE opens cupboards. She opens the fridge. The MIGRANT drops out. Frozen – a dummy again. She sees ROB at the side of the stage and runs off after him. SUGAR bursts out of the cupboard and aims his gun at STUART. Slowly, STUART raises his head to look at SUGAR. For a moment there's a look of contempt – then he takes in the rifle. He looks away. Then back. It's still trained on him. Slowly, he gets up from the table and starts to move. Then runs – up into the audience. SUGAR chases him.

ALL: Fill your home with bits of plastic
All your friends think it's fantastic
Living life inside a flash-pack
If you don't like it – send it back.

Always have more than you need –
If you buy one, you'll get one free.
If you buy two, you'll get a third one –
And ten per cent extra just for fun.

SUGAR brings STUART through the audience. He has the gun to his head.

STUART: (*On mic.*) I think he wants me to sing the song.

(*Sings.*) Call me greedy – call me vain,
But let me tell you – you're the same.
I think I'm misunderstood –
Lucky, yes, but surely good.

Tsunami, Band Aid – I support them,
Red Nose, Pudsey – I bought them.
I've done my bit for everyone else
Now let me think about myself.

Finally, CATHERINE catches ROB and pulls the cat off. CATHERINE goes to change into the TREACLE costume. ROB literally has no face left. Just a bloody mess. He staggers around – he cannot see.

ALL: And someone else dies –
A four-slice toaster –
So someone else dies –
Ceramic coasters.
When someone else dies –
A bubble blower.
Then someone else dies –
A ride-on mower.
So someone else dies –
Silicone implants.
When someone else dies –
Musical underpants.
Then someone else dies –
A virtual pet.
So someone else dies –
A pic-nic set.
When someone else dies –
A massaging chair.
And someone else dies –
Transplanted hair.

As the song continues, we hear a voice over.

VOICE OVER: If you feel you've been affected by any of the issues in tonight's performance, then do something about it.

The MIGRANT on the table leaps up and runs out into the audience, half-eaten.

Because you're everso everso close this time
To feeling really almost fine.
Because you're everso everso close this time
To feeling really almost fine.
You're really nearly really happy
Nearly really really happy.
Really nearly happy.

The song ends suddenly. As it does, SUGAR pulls his head off to reveal that he is the ACTOR PLAYING ALEX. As he speaks, ROB appears at the side of the stage, dabbing the mess that was his face with a spotted hanky. The ACTOR PLAYING ALEX tells us the end of his story – we recognise it.

THE ACTOR PLAYING ALEX: So the American guy goes over to the body on the bed – and it's the girl whose apartment it is. We wake her up and then she sees the door leaning up against this cavernous hole I've made, and she gets really pissed off. And we really want to go now. And she wants us out of there. She's demanding that we leave.

And I would have done, I would have gone. If I'd had anywhere to go.

They all exit. Messily.

ALSO AVAILABLE FROM OBERON BOOKS

SOAP
BY SARAH WOODS   ISBN 1 84002 510 7 £7.99

HILDA BY MARIE NDIAYE
TRANSLATED BY SARAH WOODS   ISBN 1 84002 309 0 £7.99

TRIPS
BY SARAH WOODS   ISBN 1 84002 110 1 £7.99

GRACE / CAKE
BY SARAH WOODS   ISBN 1 84002 425 9 £9.99

OTHER HANDS
BY LAURA WADE   ISBN 1 84002 650 2 £8.99

COLDER THAN HERE
BY LAURA WADE   ISBN 1 84002 471 2 £7.99

BREATHING CORPSES
BY LAURA WADE   ISBN 1 84002 546 8 £7.99

ADRENALIN HEART
BY GEORGIA FITCH   ISBN 1 84002 327 9 £7.99

FALLING
BY SHELLEY SILAS   ISBN 1 84002 328 7 £7.99

CALCUTTA KOSHER
BY SHELLEY SILAS   ISBN 1 84002 430 5 £7.99

MERCY FINE
BY SHELLEY SILAS   ISBN 1 84002 637 5 £8.99

KINGFISHER BLUE
BY LIN COGHLAN   ISBN 1 84002 576 X £7.99

COMPACT FAILURE
BY JENNIFER FARMER   ISBN 1 84002 518 2 £7.99

GUANTANAMO: HONOR BOUND TO DEFEND FREEDOM
BY VICTORIA BRITTAIN & GILLIAN SLOVO   ISBN 1 84002 474 7 £7.99

BEHZTI (DISHONOUR)
BY GURPREET KAUR BHATTI   ISBN 1 84002 522 0 £7.99

**For information on these and other plays and books published by
Oberon, or for a free catalogue, listing all titles and cast breakdowns,
visit our website**

www.oberonbooks.com

info@oberonbooks.com • 020 7607 3637